TEDDY KOLLEK

Builder of Jerusalem

Teddy Kollek

TEDDY KOLLEK

Builder of Jerusalem

Abraham Rabinovich

Illustrated with Photographs and Maps

THE JEWISH PUBLICATION SOCIETY
Philadelphia • Jerusalem

The Jewish Publication Society wishes to thank Teddy Kollek and the
Israel Government Press Office for providing the photographs reproduced
in this book.

First edition   All rights reserved

Manufactured in the United States of America

Library of Congress Cataloging-in-Publication Data

Rabinovich, Abraham.
Teddy Kollek, builder of Jerusalem
p. cm. — (JPS young biography series)
Includes bibliographical references.
Summary: Narrates the life of the Budapest-born Zionist who was
mayor of Jerusalem from 1965 until 1993.
ISBN 0 – 8276 – 0559 – 5 (cloth)
ISBN 0 – 8276 – 0561 – 7 (pbk.)
1. Kollek, Teddy, 1911 – — Juvenile literature. 2. Mayors —
Jerusalem — Biography — Juvenile literature. 3. Jerusalem —
Biography — Juvenile literature. [1. Kollek, Teddy, 1911 – .
2. Jews — Jerusalem — Biography.] I. Title. II. Series.
DS109.86.K64R33 1995
956.94, 42054, 092 — dc20
[B]   95 – 15871
                                                          CIP
                                                          AC
1 2 3 4 5 6 7 8 9 10

CONTENTS

1	City on Fire	1
2	The Early Years	7
3	Pioneer	29
4	Mission to Europe	39
5	Secret Agent	47
6	Farewell to Ein Gev	55
7	Gunrunner	61
8	Washington Interlude	69
9	Mayor	83
10	United Jerusalem	91
11	The Last Race	107
	Important Dates in the Life of Teddy Kollek	119
	Index	121

1

City on Fire

Teddy Kollek stood at the window on the upper floor of City Hall watching his city being blown apart. Columns of dirty gray smoke rose into the sky as artillery shells exploded across Jerusalem. The sound of the explosions mixed with the popping sound of rifles and the clatter of machine guns nearby. No one could be seen on the streets.

Teddy Kollek was mayor of Jerusalem. This morning — June 5, 1967 — he had been at his desk just after eight o'clock when the sirens had gone off, their up-and-down wail drowning out the sound of traffic on busy Jaffa Road below. The mayor had leaned across his large desk and turned on the radio. It was common to have a radio at work because dramatic events were often happening in Israel.

Within seconds, an announcer interrupted the regular program. Israel was at war, he said. A heavy battle was under way in the south against Egypt. The announcer then began reading code words — "Falling Leaves," "Night Bird," "Early Start." Each code referred to an army unit. The army was made up mainly of civilians who trained as soldiers one month a year and were available in times of emergency. Around the country, men hearing the code word of their unit dropped whatever they were doing and headed for army camps to receive their uniforms and weapons.

Jerusalem's schoolchildren were in their classrooms when the sirens sounded. As they had often done in practice drills, elementary school students formed lines and followed their teachers down to basement shelters. High school students headed instead for hospitals and other emergency stations to which they had been assigned as helpers.

The war that had broken out with Egypt was two hundred miles away, and the mayor prayed that it would not reach Jerusalem. The city shared a border with an Arab country, Jordan, but there was hope that Jordan would choose to keep out of the war. For two hours it did. Shortly after 10:00 A.M., however, the sound of explosions and gunfire all across the city told the mayor that Jerusalem was now on the front line. Looking out the window, he could see that the shells made no distinction between rich neighborhoods and poor. Brush fires set off by the explosions sent up huge clouds of smoke. From the mayor's window it looked as though half the city was burning.

"I'm going down," he said to his secretary.

"Take care, Teddy," she said.

Although he was fifty-six years old, he was still called Teddy by everybody — from street cleaners to ambassadors.

To find the war, he did not have to go farther than fifty yards from his office. Jerusalem was a divided city. Its western half was part of Israel, its eastern half part of Jordan. The two halves of the city had been separated by barbed wire and minefields for nineteen years, but until this morning they had existed in relative peace alongside each other. It was the peace not of good neighbors but of enemies who pretended the other side was not there. From certain rooftops, it was possible to look into the other Jerusalem. But high walls had been built along most of the border against the possibility of snipers shooting into streets or windows.

The mayor's office lay almost on the border. Emerging onto the empty street with the sounds of war all about him, he ran crouched toward the sound of shooting. There was an old apartment house between City Hall and the nearest Jordanian machine gun position. The building was inhabited by poor families, and the mayor was concerned about how they were holding up. He ran halfway across an open square and took shelter behind a parked car. The sound of gunfire, loud and frightening, echoed off the sides of the buildings, making it impossible to tell where the shooting was coming from. Looking around to reassure himself that there were no Jordanian guns in view, he continued his run and reached the apartment house.

The residents were sitting quietly on the floor of the lobby. The old building had no basement that could serve as a shelter, and the lobby was the one place offering a measure of protection since it had no windows. Soldiers were guarding the doorway. An officer came forward to report to the mayor that all families had been evacuated from their apartments and that soldiers were using some of the upstairs rooms as firing positions. The residents were greatly relieved to see the familiar figure of the mayor. "What's going to happen to us, Teddy?" an old woman asked.

For an hour they had been sitting within a few dozen yards of the Jordanian gun positions with a terrible racket of gunfire all about them. They all imagined themselves being massacred.

"It's going to be all right," said Teddy, walking among them. "Our army is strong and doing well. We will get you out of here as soon as we can."

The very fact that the mayor had been able to reach them was reassuring. Mounting the stairs, he looked through the door of an apartment and saw a soldier standing on a bed preparing to fire a bazooka out the window. Through the window curtains, a Jordanian gun position could be seen on the ancient walls of the Old City just across the road. The soldier turned to the mayor and motioned him to move away. As Teddy walked down the stairs, he heard the bazooka fire.

For the rest of the day, the mayor toured border

areas to encourage residents trapped in their homes. At one point his car was hit by rifle fire but he was not injured.

After two days of battle, the guns in Jerusalem fell silent. Israel had won the war, and the Jordanian half of the city was in its hands. As Kollek crossed the former border for the first time, an exhausted soldier sleeping with his back against the wall looked up at the sound of approaching footsteps and recognized the mayor.

"We've given you a bigger city, Teddy," he called out.

"Yes," answered the mayor, "and a bigger headache."

Not even he, however, could yet appreciate the size of the headache. Two peoples who had been trying to kill each other were about to become neighbors, free to walk in each other's streets. The police and the army would be on hand to provide protection, but in the long run, the city's Jewish and Arab residents would have to make peace between themselves.

In the transformation of Jerusalem from a battlefield into a united city, the mayor would be the central figure. As it happened, it would have been difficult to find anyone better suited by his personality and his life experience to guide Jerusalem and its people through this difficult change than the man everyone called Teddy.

2

The Early Years

Teddy Kollek was born on May 27, 1911, in a small village named Nagyvaszony overlooking the Danube River near Budapest. His earliest memories would be of the lights of boats passing on the river at night. His father was a business executive working for the Rothschilds, the wealthiest Jewish family in the world. "As rich as Rothschild" was an expression people would use when they wanted to suggest that someone was as rich as could possibly be. The Kolleks themselves were not rich in that way, but they lived in a comfortable home, filled with books and glass objects that Teddy's father liked to collect. Teddy was the first child. His brother, Paul, was not born until eleven years after him, so Teddy spent his earliest years as an only child.

His father, Alfred, was a handsome man who had been an athlete in his younger days. He liked to dress well and once or twice a year went to the best tailors to have a new suit fitted. He was generous in buying gifts for his son but was a strict disciplinarian. Teddy turned out to be a poor student, and this angered his father, who was himself the son of a schoolteacher. Mr. Kollek believed that success in school was important for success in life. Sometimes the elder Kollek, returning late from work, woke Teddy to question him about his poor schoolwork. Once or twice he ended the discussion by smacking Teddy. His father would not permit him to have a bicycle for fear that he would be run over by a streetcar or one of the horse-drawn carriages that raced through the streets. Teddy's relationship with his father was rather formal, but he learned from him many traits that he would himself adopt as an adult. These included attention to detail, hard work, and loyalty to his people. He would also become a collector like his father.

Teddy's relationship with his mother, Rachel, was much warmer. She was thirteen years younger than his father and the daughter of a well-to-do merchant. Several members of her family owned small estates in the country, which Teddy and his parents would periodically visit. Mrs. Kollek was a homebody who liked to sew and bake. She and her husband would frequently attend afternoon tea parties to raise money for Jewish charities. The family was active in the Jewish community in whatever city they happened to be living and went to synagogue on Jewish holidays and occasionally on Saturdays. But they did not observe the Sabbath except for the lighting of candles by Mrs. Kollek on Friday evenings.

On Sundays, relatives would gather either at the home of Teddy's parents or at the home of Mr. Kollek's brother, Emil. Every Passover Teddy and his parents would take a six-hour train ride through an area dotted with old castles to Uncle Ignatz's farm. There were cows and horses on the large farm, and Teddy loved to wander through the beautiful orchards. For holiday services, everybody in the local Jewish community, including those who lived on surrounding farms, would gather in the synagogue of the nearby town.

Teddy was only three years old when the First World War broke out, throwing the family's orderly life into turmoil. His father, as did all university graduates, served as an officer in the army of the Austro-Hungarian Empire, which fought at the side of Germany. Although the Germans would attempt to destroy the Jews in the Second World War a quarter of a century later, Jewish soldiers and officers in the First World War fought on the German side like all other citizens. When his father was called to the army, Teddy and his mother moved to Berlin, where her parents lived. From time to time his father came home from the battlefront, and Teddy and his mother stayed in the small towns where he was posted. In one such place, a village built around a monastery, Teddy spent his first year at school. But dysentery and other illnesses kept him from attending class much . Food was difficult to obtain, but Teddy's mother made great efforts to purchase chocolate or cocoa, which she thought would help cure whatever ailed him.

The end of the war brought great changes. Teddy had been born into a large empire, Austria-Hungary, made up of many lands whose inhabitants spoke different languages. It was a rich and powerful empire ruled over for sixty-eight years by Emperor Franz Josef, a bearded figure who was looked up to like a father by his people. In the middle of the war, Franz Josef died. As an army officer, Teddy's father attended the funeral and took his son along. Teddy would long remember the horse-drawn platform carrying the body of the old emperor as it moved through the streets of Vienna followed by marching soldiers. Tearful crowds lined the way as the horses and flags and troops in colorful uniforms moved by. It was as if the people sensed that the death of Franz Josef meant that the world they had known had also come to an end.

When the terrible war ended after four years, the Austro-Hungarian Empire was on the losing side. The United States and its allies on the winning side decided to break up the empire into several small countries. One of these was Austria, and it was in its capital, Vienna, that the Kollek family settled after the war. The elder Kolleks had married there, and it was the city they had always called home. Teddy was seven years old. Although Vienna was now the capital of only a small country, it still showed signs of having been Franz Josef's capital. It was full of grand buildings and wide boulevards, recalling its status as the heart of a great empire. During his half-hour walk to school, Teddy would pass walls plastered with old election posters in languages like Polish, German, Hungarian, Czech, and Croat, which had been spoken in the empire. Now the main language spoken in Austria was German.

One in every ten persons living in Vienna was Jewish, a very high percentage. The influence of the 200,000 Jews on the life of the city and the country was in fact even greater than their numbers — far greater. There have been few cities in history where Jews played so central a role as they did in Vienna in the early part of the twentieth century. When Teddy's grandparents were children, hardly any Jews were able to get government jobs and few were accepted to university. There were almost no Jewish doctors or lawyers. Many Jews even chose to convert to Christianity so that they could study at university and get good jobs. The great majority of Jews lived in small towns where they owned tiny shops or worked at trades like boot-making and tailoring.

When discrimination against Jews officially ended in 1867, they leaped at the opportunities opened to them and streamed into the big cities and to the universities. By the time Teddy's parents married in 1910, the Jews were the most powerful force in the cultural life of Vienna. Half the doctors and almost three quarters of the lawyers in the city were Jewish. Three quarters of the best-known writers, most of the journalists, and the most famous playwrights were Jews. In science, music, and many other fields they were equally prominent. The city was famous for its elegant cafés where educated people came to read newspapers and chat. Here, too, Jews were the most prominent group.

The best-known Viennese Jew was Sigmund Freud, a doctor who came to realize that the mental problems many adults have are often the result of things that happened to them as children. It was Freud who founded the practice of psychoanalysis.

Another famous Viennese Jew was Theodor Herzl, a journalist who believed that the Jewish people, in order to live normal lives, must have a country of their own like other peoples. He founded the Zionist movement, whose aim was to see a Jewish state established in the land where the Jews had lived in biblical times. Zion had been one of the names for Jerusalem in the time of the Bible, and its use by the new movement symbolized the desire of Jews to return to their ancient land, now called Palestine. In fifty years, the movement would in fact bring about the creation of the State of Israel. Mr. and Mrs. Kollek named their son after Theodor Herzl but preferred to call the child by the shortened form of the name. Teddy, when he grew up, would agree with their choice and always resisted attempts to call him Theodor.

The Kolleks were the only Jewish family in their apartment building. Teddy did not go to a Jewish school, but his parents had grown up in Orthodox homes and they followed traditional Jewish practices. Only kosher food was eaten at home. Mrs. Kollek belonged to a group of Jewish women who visited the sick in hospitals. Mr. Kollek received Zionist magazines, which Teddy sometimes thumbed through.

The tremendous success the Jews had achieved in Vienna in such a short time brought them many enemies. There was hardly a Jewish child, including Teddy, who at some point was not attacked by anti-Semites. The mayor of Vienna was himself a well-known hater of Jews. The Jews reacted to this rejection in different ways. Some chose to move to other countries, usually the United States. Many continued to see their future in Austria and supported political parties that were not anti-Semitic. Some became Zionists, whose goal was to eventually leave for Palestine.

At age eleven, Teddy Kollek became a Zionist without at first knowing much about what that meant. A boy his age who lived across the street, Efra Schallinger, the son of the Kollek family doctor, suggested one day that Teddy join him at a meeting of his Zionist club. Teddy went along and found it fun. They sang Hebrew songs and were told stories by the group leader about Palestine, a neglected land that Jewish pioneers had begun to build up. For some years now, the youth leader told them, small groups of Jews from Europe had been sailing to Palestine to establish farming colonies. Groups were now organizing in Austria too, and young men and women in the Zionist movement were going off to training farms to learn how to plant crops and look after cows. Teddy, who loved

Uncle Ignatz's farm, thought it a first-class idea to be a farmer. His parents gave him their permission to become a member of the club.

It would be years before he was old enough to go to a training farm, but meanwhile there were the youth club's get-togethers two or three times a week, summer camps, and lots of hiking in the country. Sunday was the main activity day. The boys in the club would set up tents alongside one of the area lakes and spend the day swimming and boating. There were fifteen boys in Teddy's group, and their greatest dream was to have a folding canoe that they could carry with them from the clubhouse to the lake. Teddy was the first to do something about it. The occasion was his bar mitzvah. The religious ceremony was held in the main synagogue in Vienna. The chief rabbi of the city made a speech that deeply moved the bar mitzvah boy. Afterward, the guests assembled at the Kollek home for a party.

As was the custom, Teddy got up at the end to recite a speech he had memorized. He spoke of his hopes and, as bar mitzvah boys always do, thanked his parents for having raised him the way they did. When he finished his speech, which he had prepared with the help of his religious teacher, Teddy did not sit down. To the surprise of the teacher and his parents, he told the guests that he would like to say a few more words. He belonged to a youth movement, he said, and what he and his friends most wanted was a folding canoe. Since the guests were all giving him presents anyway, Teddy asked if they would mind adding a bit of money to help the group buy a canoe. Later in life he would raise many millions of dollars for different causes by making speeches around the world, but this was his first attempt at it and one of the most satisfying. One of his friends at the bar mitzvah was inspired by Teddy's courage to do the same thing at his own bar mitzvah a week later. Soon the group had its own canoe.

Teddy was a natural leader—he was good-looking, had a good sense of humor, and felt comfortable in almost any situation and with almost any kind of people. By feeling comfortable, he made others around him comfortable. He was a good skater and skier, and although he was never a very good student, he read lots of books. Among his favorites were translations of works by American writers Mark Twain and Edgar Allan Poe into German, his native language. He often went to the theater and opera, waiting in line for hours before performances to buy cheap standing-room tickets in the upper balcony.

All his close friends were Jews. He did not dislike non-Jews and got along well with them when he met them, but he had a sense that his fate was linked to the Jewish people. Once, when he fell ill, his mother took him to a resort in the high mountains of the Alps for a few months, which was the way certain illnesses were treated before there were modern medicines like penicillin. Most of the people at the resort were non-Jews, and Teddy found it easy to mix with them. One or two even became his girlfriends during this time, and there was a well-known poet with whom he

15

Teddy (left) at age fourteen on holiday with his parents and brother Paul at a Karlsbad resort in 1925. (Courtesy of Teddy Kollek)

had interesting conversations. But Teddy had no interest in making contact with any of them again when he returned to Vienna.

More and more of his time was spent with the Zionist youth movement. In the beginning it had been for him little more than a social club where he could be with his friends. Over time it became more serious. The idea of leaving Austria to settle in Palestine, once only a far away thought, was now a real choice. Some of the boys and girls at this point dropped out of the movement as they came to realize that they did not want to leave the country where they had grown up or leave their families and friends. However, for those who remained in the organization the planned move to Palestine steadily became the most real thing in their lives. Teddy and his friends had no intention of going to Palestine to become businessmen or doctors like their parents. It was their intention to become farmers and laborers.

The idea of Zionism was to rebuild not only Zion but also the Jewish people. In the two thousand years since they had lived in their ancient homeland the Jews had been guests in other people's lands. They had had to learn to live by their wits and they had been quite successful. But very few were farmers. In many countries Jews had not been permitted to own land. Even where they were allowed, few now chose to do so. More and more Jews were studying at universities and taking up professions that required great skills but not physical labor. The Zionists said that if the Jews were to become a normal nation they must return not only to their homeland but to farming and physical labor as well. The songs the Zionist youths sang and the stories they told were frequently about farm life in the Jewish homeland.

Whenever visitors from one of the Jewish farming colonies in Palestine came to Vienna, Teddy and his friends went to meet them. Many of these colonies were kibbutzim. These were very different from the farms or farming villages of Europe. In a kibbutz everyone shared equally in the work and everyone got the same payment. No one on a kibbutz would be richer or poorer than anyone else there. Many Jews going to Palestine were settling in cities like Tel Aviv or Jerusalem, but the ones who sought the toughest challenges went to the kibbutzim. These colonies were often set up in wilderness areas and on the dangerous borders. Being in a kibbutz meant performing backbreaking work clearing rocks and drying swamps before it was even possible to plant crops. It meant risking sickness or death from malaria and other diseases that were widespread in these areas. It meant facing danger of attacks from Arabs who were fighting the Jews for the land. In the end, whether or not there was to be a Jewish state in Palestine depended in large part on the kibbutzim. What the Zionist movement most needed was young men and women willing to live as pioneers in great hardship in order to farm the land and defend it.

Thousands of Zionist pioneers from Poland and Russia stopped off for a day or two in Vienna on their way to Palestine during these years. The Zionist movement in the city bought a building to serve as their dormitory. Teddy and his friends would often visit there. The pioneers, who greeted them warmly, were only a few years older than the Viennese youths and readily shared with them their view of the future.

Teddy became so involved in the Zionist movement that he decided to quit high school in his senior year and go to a training farm to prepare himself for life in Palestine. His parents were very upset, but they could not persuade him to change his mind.

At the farm there were cows and vineyards. Teddy and other trainees were once given the job of filling barrels in the basement with wine. When no one was looking, they decided to try the wine. They liked the taste and tasted some more. They did not feel anything as long as they were in the basement, but the moment they went outside into the fresh air they became so dizzy they could hardly stand. When Teddy finished the farming course, his parents persuaded him to return to high school and finish his education. They did not object to his going to Palestine, they said, but if he wanted to be useful there, he had to complete his basic education first. Teddy would never be sure whether they told him that only to get him back to school or whether they really approved of his going to Palestine. Perhaps they accepted the idea of his going because they sensed that the anti-Semitism in Austria meant bad times ahead.

If he was to go to Palestine, however, his parents preferred that he become a businessman or executive there rather than a farmer. Teddy had long arguments with his parents about this and finally gave in to his father's suggestion that he take a job at a big steel plant owned by the Rothschilds in order to gain some practical experience. Teddy went off to the plant in Czechoslovakia but became bored after a week or two. He decided to quit and work for the local Zionist organization in Czechoslovakia instead. His parents accepted his decision and sent money to help support him. He joined a Jewish commune made up of young people like him. Living as though on a kibbutz, they shared whatever money they earned. In their rented house they slept six to eight in each room. Most worked in factories during the day and studied Hebrew at night. All were waiting for permission to enter Palestine. Entry was controlled by the British, who ruled the country. Only a limited number of permits were issued each year. Teddy's jobs in the commune were putting out a Zionist newspaper, organizing meetings, and organizing youth camps. He also served as a youth leader. He met with his group regularly to teach Hebrew songs and dances and talk about Palestine. It was in Czechoslovakia that Teddy fell in love for the first time. She was a pretty, sharp-tongued girl who was a member of the Zionist movement, but she showed no interest in him. Although she too would go to Palestine, they would never meet again.

His parents had not given up hope of Teddy becoming a businessman. They persuaded him after a year to go to an uncle in Germany who had a large auto-parts business. However, the same thing happened in Germany as had happened in Czechoslovakia. Teddy worked a few hours a day with his uncle but spent most of his time with the local Zionist movement. The Nazis were already on the rise in Germany, although they had not yet come to power under Hitler. It soon became apparent that the Nazis were the most dangerous anti-Semitic group of all. One day Teddy was with a group of youths when they were set upon by Nazi toughs. There was a fight and he was arrested. From the police station he was taken to a detention camp. Although it was nothing like the concentration camps to which the Nazis would later take Jews before killing them, it was unpleasant enough, and Teddy was very relieved when his uncle got him out after a few days. Teddy became involved in more fights with the Nazis. Since he was an Austrian citi-

zen and not a German, the police told him that he was
no longer welcome. Before leaving the country, Teddy
decided to visit the capital, Berlin, once more. Hitler
had just come to power, and what Teddy saw was
enough to convince him that the time had come to get
out. The streets were full of uniformed storm troopers
and Nazi flags. Teddy met with local Zionist leaders
who spoke about their fears. It was plain that something evil had happened to Germany and that terrible
times lay ahead, especially for the Jews. No one, however, could yet imagine how terrible.

Teddy, now twenty-two, did not return to Vienna
but went to a small resort in Czechoslovakia called
Karlsbad. He was becoming a popular figure in the
Zionist movement in central Europe and was asked to
help organize local Zionist groups in several areas.
Using Karlsbad as a base, he lived frugally on money
his father sent him. The resort lay on the border with
Germany, and it was possible to ski across the
unfenced frontier in winter to keep contact with
German Jews. One day a local Zionist leader invited
Teddy to his office. Sitting with him was a well-
dressed couple who looked very anxious. They were
from the German town of Chemnitz just across the
border, but from their appearance and accent it was
clear that they were not native Germans. They were
Iranian Jews who had been living in Germany for a
few years. The man was wealthy enough to have set
up textile factories in Chemnitz and he had since
become even wealthier.

That morning, however, as he and his wife arrived
outside their office they were stopped by an employee

who said that the Gestapo was waiting for them. The Gestapo was the Nazi secret police. Since he had not been born in Germany and was also a wealthy Jew, the factory owner had particular reason to fear arrest. The Germans had not yet begun their mass murders, but they were putting people away in camps for months. If the couple wished to avoid arrest, their only choice was to escape immediately, but they had left their two-year-old son at home in the care of a nanny. They assumed that the Gestapo had sent men to their home as well and would be waiting for them there. After thinking the situation over briefly, the couple telephoned relatives to ask that they bring the child and nanny to their house. Then the man and his wife headed for the border and crossed on foot through the snow. They had come straight to Karlsbad to ask the Zionist organization there for help in getting their son out. They would be willing to pay a large sum to the Zionist movement if someone could be found to do it.

Teddy agreed to try despite the danger that his arrest in Germany the year before might mean serious trouble for him if he were arrested again. That very night he took the train across the border to Chemnitz. He had a friend in the city named Xiel Federmann, a member of the local Zionist youth movement. Teddy slept over at his house and discussed with him the best way to carry out the operation. Years later, Federmann would remember the elegant black coat with fur collar worn by Teddy, who was posing as a "respectable" young businessman with a newspaper under his arm. "Teddy was fearless," Federmann would remember. "He knew what he wanted and what he could do to get it. I could see then in Teddy what Jerusalem would see years later."

The Persian couple had left a large amount of money in a safe in their house, which they asked Teddy to get. In the morning, Teddy and his friend took a taxi to the Persian couple's house on the edge of the city. It was a beautiful villa surrounded by a garden. The red seal of the Gestapo had been fixed to all the doors. This meant that it was forbidden for anyone to enter. Teddy and Xiel left the house untouched and went to the relative with whom the child was staying. The nanny, a German non-Jew, was still looking after the child. It was plain to Teddy that she could be trusted. He asked whether she would be willing to help take the boy across the border. She agreed despite the risk.

The next morning at dawn Teddy and Xiel returned to the villa. Avoiding the front entrance in case someone was watching, they made their way through the garden and reached a side door. The Persian man had given Teddy the key. He broke the Gestapo seal and unlocked the door. Inside they quickly found the safe and opened it with another key. There was a lot of money inside but it was in very large bills so that Teddy could fit it all inside his wallet. They shut the door behind them and rearranged the seal so that the break would not be noticed unless someone looked closely.

Moving according to the plan they had worked out, Teddy arrived at the train station five minutes before the train was to leave for the border. From another direction at the same time came Xiel's girlfriend with the boy. From a third direction came the boy's nanny with a suitcase. The nanny took the boy's hand and boarded the train with Teddy.

He had chosen to cross the border at a different point from where he had entered so that the border guards who had seen him arrive in Germany alone would not be made suspicious by seeing him depart with a child. At least as big a problem as the boy was the money he was carrying. By law, travelers were allowed to leave Germany with no more than two hundred marks, the German currency. In his wallet were tens of thousands of marks. During the hour-long ride to the border he thought about how he would respond if the guards searched him. He hoped they would not search him, but what if they did? If they found the money, he could be put in prison for a long time, particularly since he had broken the Gestapo seal and already had an arrest record. Suddenly he remembered one of the stories by Edgar Allan Poe he had read, "The Purloined Letter." In the story, police searching for a document in an apartment pull everything apart but fail to look in the most obvious place. The document had been left in an envelope on top of a desk in full view.

When the train reached the border, Teddy and the nanny got off the train with the boy and walked to the border control post. "Any money with you?" asked one of the guards. Teddy reached into his pocket and pulled out his wallet. "It's all in here," he said, holding it out. He said it calmly but he felt frightened. The guard took the wallet and tossed it on the tabletop. Another guard now came over. They asked Teddy to open the bags he and the nanny were carrying. The guards went through everything in the bags and searched their clothing. They even stuck a pin through a teddy bear the boy had been carrying to see if there was money or jewelry inside. The only object that was not searched was the wallet that was still lying on the tabletop. When the guards were done, Teddy picked up the wallet and put it back in his pocket, trying to look calm. He and the nanny passed through the border into Czechoslovakia.

With a tiny bit of the money the Persian factory owner happily gave to the Zionist movement, Teddy traveled to the eastern part of Czechoslovakia and Romania to contact young Jews there. It was his first visit to the area where some of the poorest Jews of Europe lived. They were very different from the Jews whom he had known until now. In Austria and Germany the Jews were wealthier and better educated than most non-Jews and they lived mostly in the big cities. In eastern Europe they were poor, had very little education, and lived in small towns. Instead of being doctors and lawyers, they were blacksmiths and woodcutters. Instead of driving cars, they had at best horses and wagons. To his surprise, Teddy found himself liking them. They may have seemed poor and simple compared to the Jews of Vienna, but there was something proud and natural about them. Most of the Jews of Europe, in fact, were these poor Jews of the east, millions of them. Less than ten years after Teddy's visit, almost all would be dead—murdered by the Germans in the death camps of the Holocaust.

Shortly after returning to Vienna, Teddy met the woman who would become his wife. Tamar was only seventeen, six years younger than Teddy. The daughter of a prominent rabbi, she was in her senior year of high school and had joined the Zionist movement. Teddy was her group leader. Tamar at first had a crush on another youth leader, but after a while she let Teddy walk her home at night from the group meetings. They would stand for a long time under the streetlight outside her home talking. She too was preparing herself to move to Palestine and had begun studying gardening. Although she spent more of her time working with the movement than doing school-work, she received excellent grades. This impressed Teddy, who had never managed to get high marks.

Anti-Semitism was growing steadily worse in Vienna, and the Nazi movement had arrived there too. One Sunday Teddy was watching a group of Jewish youngsters playing soccer in a park when Nazi youths came over and took away the ball. Teddy walked over to the one holding the ball, slapped him, and took the ball back. The youth was shocked. "What are you doing with those Jews?" he asked Teddy, not believing that the blond-haired young man could be Jewish himself. Teddy slapped him again. A few weeks later, the Nazi gang ambushed Teddy outside a movie house and beat him up.

The Zionist movement for a long time prevented Teddy from going to Palestine because he was needed in Europe. At a meeting of Zionist youth leaders from all over Europe, a participant from Yugoslavia, Reuven Dafni, would many years later recall being impressed by the tall young man from Vienna who carried himself easily and spoke sensibly. What he remembered most of all was how Teddy, who was standing against a wall, suddenly stopped talking in the middle of a sentence as if he were trying to find the right word.

Tamar as a young woman when Teddy first met her.
(Courtesy of Teddy Kollek)

Only when Dafni heard the sound of snoring did he realize that Teddy had gone to sleep standing up and in the middle of his own sentence. Because of the long hours he worked, Teddy managed to get very little sleep at night and made up for it by falling asleep during the day at unexpected times. It was a habit that would stay with him for the rest of his life.

In 1935, Teddy finally received permission from the Zionist movement to leave for Palestine. First, however, he was asked to go to England on a mission. He spent three months there and then returned to Vienna to take leave of his family and friends and to say goodbye to Tamar. She would follow as soon as she could. In December, he took a train for the Italian port of Trieste, where he boarded the ship that would carry him to Palestine. The name of the ship was *Jerusalem*.

3

Pioneer

Waiting for Teddy when the ship docked in Haifa was the childhood friend from across the street who had first introduced him to the Zionist movement fourteen years before, Efra Schallinger. The doctor's son had arrived several years before. He took Teddy to his kibbutz, Givat Haim, less than an hour's drive away. The ship voyage had been wonderful. There had been hundreds of pioneers aboard, young men and women on the way at last to do what they had been talking about for years and training for. Like Teddy, they had given up any idea of going to university or becoming wealthy in business. They wanted to do physical work and help build a Jewish homeland. As they sailed across the Mediterranean Sea, they gathered on the ship's deck every evening to sing Hebrew songs to the accompaniment of a harmonica. All of them felt that they were leaving their past far behind them and sailing toward a new life.

The morning after his arrival at Givat Haim, Teddy began his first workday in Palestine, helping build a house in a nearby Jewish village. The job continued late into the night. When they finished, the workers celebrated with wine and cake. In the book *For Jerusalem* he would write years later about his life, Teddy summed up this first day. "Everything around me was just as I had pictured it—the landscape, the work, and the pioneer spirit. I was home."

However, his friend's kibbutz was only a stopover for a few days. Teddy was part of a group that was to start its own kibbutz. For the young pioneers it was the most exciting thing they could hope for—to create on a rocky piece of land a new settlement that would be filled with life. Teddy joined his group at Lake Kinneret. It was the only lake in the country, but it was big enough to have been called in antiquity the Sea of Galilee. The town of Tiberias and other settlements were located on the west shore of the lake. There were no settlements at all on the east shore and only dirt roads reached there. That was where Teddy's group was to found its kibbutz. Its name would be Ein Gev, which means "waterhole spring."

The site was on the border with Syria, an Arab country that opposed the creation of a Jewish state in Palestine. The settlers had reason to fear attacks and would have to be on their guard at all times. No less dangerous were mosquitoes, which carried malaria, a disease that killed many of the pioneers in different parts of the country. Teddy would indeed come down with malaria several times, as well as typhoid fever, typhus, and several other serious diseases.

Instead of first building a new settlement and then surrounding it with a protective wall, the pioneers had developed what they called the "tower and stockade" system. Men and women from many settlements would gather at the site of a new kibbutz and in one day they would build a stockade, or wooden fence, and set up a high wooden tower from which watchmen could warn of any attacks. The pioneers would thus be protected during the settlement's construction.

At age twenty-six, Teddy surrounded by fellow pioneers in Palestine.
(Courtesy of Teddy Kollek)

This is what was done at Ein Gev. In the summer of 1937 hundreds of men and women from many settlements gathered at the site of the new kibbutz early one morning with building materials that had been prepared ahead of time. By nightfall, a high wooden fence encircled the site. In the center of the compound were several huts where members of the kibbutz—kibbutznikim, as they were called—would live. There was also a high tower with a searchlight mounted on top. When the work was done, everybody joined hands to dance around a campfire. Although exhausted from the day's work, they found the strength to sing late into the night. All shared a feeling that they had created a new point on the map that, together with other such points, would link up into a Jewish state before long.

To support themselves, the kibbutznikim did whatever work they could find, including digging up gravel and sand from the edge of the lake and selling it in Tiberias for use in building roads. Teddy joined the others in carrying two-hundred-pound sacks of gravel on his back onto boats. They had to walk up a narrow plank, trying not to fall into the water. It was less easy to keep from being seasick as the boats crossed the often stormy lake to Tiberias. The storms would sometimes come without warning. Once Teddy and another kibbutznik — Reuven Dafni, who had met

---

Teddy Kollek was one of the founders of Kibbutz Ein Gev, located on the shore of Lake Kinneret. ▸

Palestine, 1935

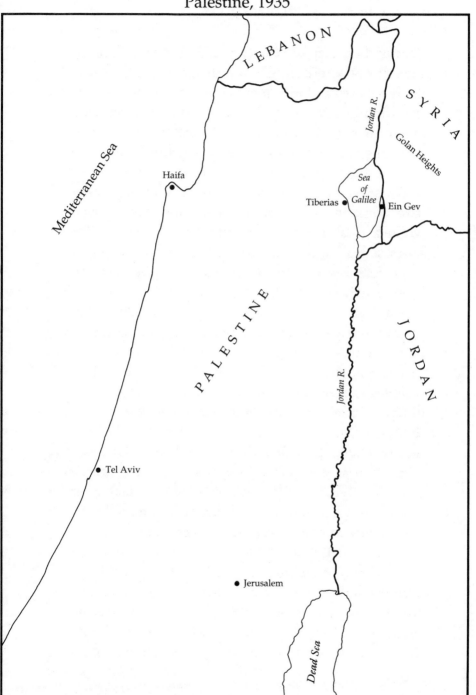

Teddy when they were both youth leaders — were in a small kayak returning from Tiberias when they suddenly saw dark clouds moving fast overhead and felt the wind beginning to rise. Two minutes after they pulled their small craft ashore the storm hit the lake, churning the water into high waves. Had they still been on the lake they would not have survived.

For several months Teddy worked as a laborer on a dam, sometimes working through the night. He also worked as a fisherman on the kibbutz boats. The boats sailed the lake at night when it was easier to catch fish, which were attracted to the light of the boats' lanterns.

Since all were considered equal, everybody on the kibbutz was paid the same amount of money whether he or she was a manager or a worker. In Ein Gev, this meant that they were all equally poor. The members received the same clothing and shoes. Only the sizes differed. For a long time there was not enough money to build huts for all the members, and most had to live on the other side of the lake in an old farm. That was where Tamar stayed when she arrived from Austria a year after Teddy. He would row across the lake after work to see her, returning before dark to help defend the kibbutz in case it was attacked at night.

Teddy and Tamar were married in Tiberias during a five-minute ceremony attended by one witness, a member of the kibbutz named Benno. Afterward, they still had to remain separated because there was no room at Ein Gev. Finally, new shacks were built and Tamar joined Teddy. There was still not enough room for everybody, so all married couples had to have a third, unmarried person sharing their one-room apartment. Teddy finally solved the problem by getting hold of a very large packing crate, cutting a door in it, and moving in with Tamar.

One shack served as the communal shower, with only a thin wood panel separating the men's section from the women's. Listening in on each other's conversations provided more entertainment than watching television would have — if there had been television.

Teddy was chosen to represent the kibbutz in its contacts with British officials. His English was better than that of the other kibbutznikim because he had spent several months in England. But no less important was his personality. He still had the same ability to make strangers feel comfortable that he had had as a youth leader. He got along easily with British officials and Arab neighbors. "He had broad knowledge of all kinds of subjects," a kibbutz member, Yossi Fogel, would remember years later. "He always found things to talk about no matter who he was talking to."

Jobs at the kibbutz were frequently rotated, and Teddy served for a while as treasurer. In this job he had to find the money to pay what the kibbutz owed. It was not an easy task. Once, a kibbutz member would recall, when Teddy had to get to the bank in Tiberias, he faced the problem of how to reach it without passing stores on the main street to which the kibbutz owed money. When he reached the edge of the town, which was located on the shores of the lake, he stripped down to a bathing suit, hid his clothes, and swam to a point where he could get to the bank without being seen by the store owners.

For some time he also served as military commander of the kibbutz. In this job he would ride a horse to nearby Arab villages in order to meet their leaders and keep up good relations. It was a task he loved, riding on the Golan Heights above Ein Gev with its beautiful views of the lake and the Galilee Hills beyond. Entering the villages, he would be received with great ceremony by the local Arab leaders. The men would sit in a circle on mattresses placed on the floor and eat from bowls in the center. The host would tear off pieces of lamb and hand them to each guest, who, with his own hands, would form a ball of the meat and rice and eat it. If there was a wedding, the men rose to dance in a circle and Teddy sometimes joined them. The women kept out of sight.

Decisions on all matters at the kibbutz, big and small, were made at the Saturday night meeting when the members gathered to discuss whatever was on their minds. At one such meeting Teddy argued that they should be eating more eggplant because it was cheap. When other members said it was just not tasty, Teddy noted that their Arab neighbors had lots of tasty recipes for eggplant. There was no reason, he argued, that the kibbutz couldn't put it on its menu more frequently.

Living conditions at Ein Gev were very difficult, and the terrible summer heat was worse than anything the kibbutznikim had ever experienced. But the life was everything Teddy had hoped for — a group of friends working together to build something new and worthwile. Each day was filled with surprises and challenges that people living ordinary lives in cities never faced. As far as Teddy was concerned, he had arrived at the home where he would spend the rest of his life. After little more than one year at Ein Gev, however, he was asked to leave the kibbutz, at least for a while. His ability to win people's confidence and to get things done had been noted by the leaders of the Zionist movement in Palestine. They had a job they wanted him to do that would take him once more to Europe and the heart of the gathering storm.

4

Mission to Europe

Europe looked much the same to Teddy in September 1938 as it had when he left it little more than two years before. But it felt very different. The growing threat of the Nazis was reflected in the tense faces on the streets and by the large number of people in uniforms. Teddy's family had barely escaped when Germany had taken over Austria a few months before. They had left behind their home and everything in it as well as almost all the money they had in the bank. As the German army marched into Vienna, the Kolleks fled to Czechoslovakia. They carried with them little more than a few pieces from Mr. Kollek's glass collection and enough money to live on for a while.

Teddy, now twenty-seven, had been asked to go to England to help train young people preparing for emigration to Palestine. He traveled first to Prague, the capital of Czechoslovakia and one of the most beautiful cities in Europe. The Germans had taken over part of Czechoslovakia too, but Prague was still free. He had a warm reunion there with his parents and young brother, Paul. If his parents had in the past hoped that Teddy would remain in Vienna, they were now thankful that he had chosen a different path. His father told him that they would follow him to Palestine before the end of the year.

After a day with his family, Teddy continued on to England, where he began training young men and women preparing for kibbutz life. Soon, however, he was asked to return to the continent on an important mission. Thousands of young people at Zionist training farms in areas now ruled by the Germans had been arrested. The Germans were still willing to let Jews go but only if other countries would take them. England agreed to accept several thousand people to work on farms and had provided permits in their names. Teddy's mission was to use the permits to get as many of the Jewish youths as he could out of the countries where they were trapped.

It was an odd feeling returning to a Vienna now under German control. Passing the house in which he had grown up, he saw a Nazi flag on the balcony. There were Nazi flags all over the city. Teddy had an appointment with a German official whose name, Adolf Eichmann, did not mean much at the time. A few years later, during the Second World War, it would be Eichmann who would organize the transportation of millions of Jews to death camps. Now, however, sitting behind his desk, he seemed to Teddy like an ordinary clerk. He kept Teddy standing but he did not shout.

"What do you want?" he asked his visitor.

Teddy said that he had entry permits from England for hundreds of Jewish youths. Eichmann asked a few questions and then said that the youths would be given permission to leave. The boys and girls whom Teddy had come to rescue would arrive in England just before the beginning of the war and their lives would be saved.

Teddy himself, after ten months abroad, was back at his kibbutz when the war broke out. But within a year the Zionist movement asked him to return to England once again. A representative of the Zionist movement in Palestine was needed to stay in contact with the Jewish population there, and Teddy had both the language skills and the personality for the job. This time, he decided, he would not leave Tamar behind. Because of the war they could not fly directly to England across Europe. Instead they had to take a very long, roundabout route down to South Africa in a seaplane that could land on rivers and lakes. Sometimes the pilot flew low to permit them to look at the elephants and other wild animals. In South Africa they boarded a ship for England. The entire trip, which today takes five hours by air, took them fifty days.

England was in the middle of a terrible war. Every night German planes dropped bombs on its major cities. When the sirens sounded, families gathered together and went down to shelters. In London, most people went into the underground, which is what the British call their subway. Many took their bedding with them and slept the night. Often they could feel the ground rocking as bombs exploded overhead. When they went up the stairs to the street in the morning, they would sometimes find it covered with glass and the rubble of houses that had been blasted apart. The Kolleks were amazed at the calmness with which the British took the blitz, as this period of bombing was called. They seemed to regard it like a bad storm that would pass in time. This ability to endure hardships without complaining was one that Teddy would always admire.

It was in England that he first got to know David Ben-Gurion, the leader of the Zionist movement. Ben-Gurion would become the first prime minister of Israel and a central figure in Teddy's life. As a boy, Teddy had heard Ben-Gurion talk at large Zionist conferences, but he had never before met him. In their first meetings Teddy was not much impressed by the small man with the unruly white hair and high-pitched voice. Unlike other Zionist leaders who had the ability to give beautiful speeches in English and to carry on charming conversations at dinner tables, Ben-Gurion seemed to have extreme opinions and used impolite language. He had no interest in charming people, and he often held ideas that were in opposition to everyone else's. As Teddy got to know him, however, he saw that Ben-Gurion's ideas usually proved right. He had the ability to see beyond the situation at the moment and to predict how things were likely to develop. One of his ideas, for instance, was that if the Jews in Palestine wanted to have their own state they would have to fight for it. And for this they would have to build up their military strength. This differed from the opinion of most Zionist leaders, who believed that whether or not a Jewish state would be created was entirely up to the leaders of England, the United States, and perhaps other countries.

Nevertheless, Ben-Gurion recognized the importance of obtaining public support in England and particularly in America. That was the reason he had come to England and shortly afterward sailed for New York. Ben-Gurion was convinced that American Jews — the largest body of Jews in the world — would have a valuable role to play through their influence on their government. The United States was the most powerful country in the world, and its position would be crucial for the Zionist cause. At that time the American Jewish community had very little influence, but within a few years this would change.

Another great Zionist leader whom Teddy got to know in London was Chaim Weizmann. A Russian-born scientist, Weizmann during the First World War had developed a new way to produce explosives that greatly helped the British war effort. Weizmann was praised for his achievements by the British government and came to know many of its leaders very well. Unlike Ben-Gurion, he was a charming man who was able to quietly persuade people, even unsympathetic people, that the Jews had a right to their own state just as other people did. It was mainly thanks to Weizmann that the British government issued a declaration supporting a Jewish homeland in Palestine.

Chaim Weizmann (center), the future president of Israel, and Teddy (left), overlooking Lake Kinneret in 1944. (Courtesy of Teddy Kollek)

By providing a legal basis for Jews to settle in Palestine, this declaration helped open the way to the creation of Israel less than thirty years later.

It was in England that Teddy had his first close contacts with the world of secret agents. Among the British officials he met were members of the intelligence services, whose job it was to know as much as possible about the world around them. Any government making decisions depends to a large extent on intelligence information about potential enemies and also about friends — how strong these countries are, which people are important, what they may be intending to do. The information sometimes comes from spies, sometimes from books and newspapers, sometimes from conversations at a dinner table. Just as he had found it easy to talk to young people during his days as a Zionist youth leader, Teddy found it easy to talk to intelligence agents and to make his own intelligence observations that would be useful to the Zionist movement.

After a year in England, Teddy and Tamar made the long round-trip back to Palestine through Africa. They returned to their friends at Ein Gev and to the beautiful lake that they had often thought about during their absence. Returning to the quiet kibbutz was a tremendous change after the nightly bombings and the hectic activity of London. But the quiet life would not last long for Teddy. Within a few weeks, he was asked to come up to Jerusalem to meet with officials of the Jewish Agency. The organization, headed by Ben-Gurion, was the unofficial government of the Jewish people in Palestine. The real government in Palestine was run by the British. It was the British who collected taxes and built roads and kept a police force. But the Jews, who hoped one day to have their own state, had set up the Agency to look after their own affairs. It operated on two levels, one open and one secret. On the open level, the Agency ran Jewish schools, set up kibbutzim and other kinds of farming communities, and looked after Jewish immigrants. On the secret level, it was training an underground army — the Haganah — for the war with the Arabs that was expected to break out someday. The Arabs did not want a Jewish state in Palestine but instead wanted an Arab state.

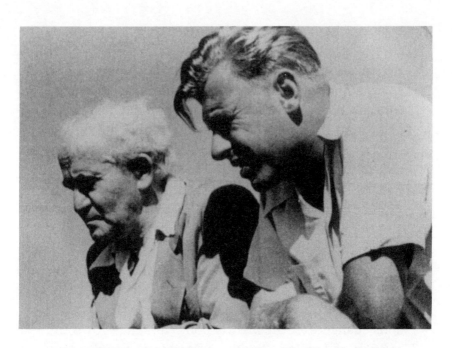

*Prime Minister David Ben-Gurion and Teddy share a
moment together at Ein Gev.
(Courtesy of Teddy Kollek)*

As part of this secret world, the Agency had set up
an intelligence organization of its own to find out
what it could about the Arab side and about the
British. Because of Teddy's experience in England, his
contacts with British intelligence, and his ability to
speak English well, he was invited for a conversation
with leaders of the Agency's intelligence organization.
They asked the young kibbutznik to forget his ambi-
tions to be a farmer, at least for a while, and to join the
organization as an intelligence officer. Teddy could
not refuse. From now on he would be at the center of
one of the most dramatic stories of our time — the
creation of the State of Israel.

5

Secret Agent

Teddy did not have to hide behind trees to spy on people in his new job as an intelligence officer. Although intelligence work involved finding out information about the other side, Teddy found that this usually could be done through pleasant talks over meals with British officials. Most of these officials were also in intelligence work, and they could exchange much information with Teddy.

As rulers of Palestine, the British served as referees of sorts between the Jews and Arabs. The Jews wanted Palestine, or at least part of it, to become a Jewish state. The Arabs strongly opposed this. The British tried to keep the Jews and Arabs from fighting each other. Some of the British officials preferred the Arabs. Some preferred the Jews. Some preferred neither. It was Teddy's job to get to know who was who, to try to understand what the British planned to do in the country, and to present the Jewish side of things to their officials. It was a job for which Teddy was perfectly suited. He liked people in general, and he liked the British in particular. Many other Palestinian Jews disliked or feared the British, whom they knew only as soldiers. Teddy had been to England and had come to admire the British as a people. It was thus easy for him to make friends with the British officials and to establish a trusting relationship that lasted for years. Tamar had remained at the kibbutz, so Teddy did a lot of dining out in Jerusalem, often with British officials.

The war against Germany gave the Jews and British a common enemy. The British agreed to a proposal by the Jewish leadership to drop dozens of Jewish agents by parachute into German-held areas in Europe. The Palestinian Jews wanted to make contact with their fellow Jews in Hungary and other countries and to help organize escape if possible. The British wanted information that these parachutists, who spoke the local languages, could give them. Thirty-six parachutists, some of them women, were dropped behind German lines from British aircraft. Not all returned.

The war was at its height in 1943 when Teddy received a new assignment. He was asked to move to Istanbul, the major city in Turkey, where he would join a small team trying to make contact with the Jews remaining in Europe. Turkey was a neutral country on the edge of Europe, and since it was at war with neither the Germans nor the Allies — as Britain, the United States, and the Soviet Union were known —

both sides operated from there. Istanbul was full of secret agents trying to spy on each other. In any restaurant, German agents might be sitting at one table, British agents at another, and agents from other countries in between. However, there was little violence. Since Istanbul was an important listening post for everybody, no side wanted to ruin it by creating unnecessary tensions.

Teddy joined three other Palestinian Jewish agents already working in Istanbul. The three had succeeded in making contacts with Jewish communities in European countries under German rule. In some cases it was possible to reach people there by telephone since connections continued to exist between neutral Turkey and the German-occupied areas. In most places in Europe, however, Jews could no longer reach telephones, and contact was maintained by agents who traveled between Turkey and these countries. These were almost all German double agents, that is, agents who worked for both sides. The Nazis knew of this but permitted the system to continue because it enabled them to read the messages sent by the Jews and to keep track of what was going on. But the Istanbul group also managed to do things that the Germans did not know about, like sending in diamonds hidden in toothpaste tubes so that a few Jews might be able to buy their way out or at least buy food. Most important, perhaps, was the sense that it gave to some trapped Jews that Jews outside the Nazi-held areas knew about their fate and were trying to do something about it. Small numbers of Jews were able to be smuggled out to Turkey, where Teddy's group cared for them and moved them on to Palestine.

The picture emerging from Europe about the fate of the Jews was at first difficult to believe. It had been known for some time that the Germans were placing Jews in large concentration camps and even killing many. But the overall situation was not clear. As the small group in Istanbul put together the reports they were getting from people who managed to escape the concentration camps and from other sources, a terrifying picture began to take shape. The Germans were murdering all the Jews under their control — men, women, and children. They were operating according to a clear plan. First the Jews were rounded up from wherever they lived. Some were placed in city neighborhoods, called ghettos, which were surrounded by walls so that no one could escape. Others were transported to concentration camps where they lived in crowded huts. Every day trains carried Jews across Europe from these places to death camps. Here they were taken in groups to buildings where they were told to undress and enter large shower rooms. Instead of water, poison gas came out of the overhead pipes. The bodies were burned in furnaces. More than six million Jews, one third of all the Jews in the world, lived in countries under German control, and the Germans were intending to kill them all.

Teddy and his colleagues were sickened by these reports. They were the first persons outside the Nazi-occupied areas to understand the nature of the Holocaust, as the murder of the six million would come to be called. Their feeling of helplessness was terrible. They wrote reports to Jerusalem and began to send letters to important people all over the world in the hope of raising an outcry that might make the Germans stop the killings. But nothing happened.

One night Teddy took home with him a young man who had just reached Istanbul from Poland, where he had escaped from one of the death camps. The young Jew had a shaven head and was so thin that his bones could be seen. He hardly spoke, and when Teddy offered him food, he shook his head, even though it was plain that he had been denied food for a long time. Finally he ate several bowls of soup. Although he spoke very little of what had happened to him, his dark eyes told a terrible tale. For Teddy, nothing he would ever hear about the Holocaust would let him feel its horror more than this meeting with the silent survivor. Within a few days, the young man was put on a train heading toward Palestine and a new life.

Teddy's job was to maintain contact with British and American intelligence officers in Istanbul. Officially, he was in Istanbul as a reporter for the *Ein Gev Diary*. The Turks had no way of knowing that there was no such newspaper, but they assumed in any case that all foreigners were spies of one sort or another. Once, in a hotel lobby, a German agent who believed Teddy to be a German came up to chat with him. Teddy made it clear that he had made a mistake and the agent hastily walked away.

The four Palestinian Jews rented two apartments in the center of town and were looked after by a local

Jewish woman who cleaned and cooked for them. They generally avoided going to restaurants so as not to be seen too often — there was no way of knowing who would notice them. One of the few times Teddy permitted himself to go to a restaurant — the best one in town — he saw the German ambassador sitting at a crowded table nearby.

Teddy returned to Jerusalem after half a year. Some time after his departure, a Jew named Yoel Brand arrived in Istanbul with a remarkable story. He had come from Hungary, which was occupied by the Germans. He had in fact arrived in a German airplane. Teddy's former comrades in Istanbul had been notified by telephone from Hungary that he was coming. One of them met Brand at the airport and drove him to an apartment where the rest of the group was waiting. Brand told them he had a message from Adolf Eichmann — the same Nazi whom Teddy had met in Vienna a few years before. Eichmann was now in charge of organizing the shipment of Jews from all over Europe to the death camps. Since most of the Jews under Nazi control had already been killed, Hungary contained the largest remaining group of Jews and he had therefore moved his headquarters there. Brand was one of the leaders of the Hungarian Jewish community. A few days before, he had been summoned to Eichmann's office. "We want to make a deal with the Allies," Eichmann told him. If the Allies could supply Germany with ten thousand trucks as well as other goods, the Germans would not send the Hungarian Jews to the death camps. Brand would be permitted to leave for neutral Istanbul, where he would pass on the offer to the Allies through the Palestinian Jews whom the Germans knew to be operating there. Eichmann gave Brand ten days during which he would stop the shipment of Jews. If Brand did not return after that period with an agreement from the Allies, Eichmann would begin sending Jews to their death once more and at an even faster pace.

It was a breathtaking offer. Instead of the few Jews who had been snatched to safety in the previous two years, here was a chance to save hundreds of thousands. But would the Allies agree to give the Germans trucks that could be used in their war effort? One member of the group, Venya Pomerantz, was chosen to go back to Jerusalem and report on the offer to Ben-Gurion. One of Teddy's British intelligence friends in Istanbul informed him by telephone that Pomerantz was coming. It was late at night when Pomerantz arrived in Jerusalem and headed for his kibbutz, Ramat Rachel, just outside the city. He found Teddy waiting for him there. Pomerantz had not planned to meet Ben-Gurion until the next morning, but Teddy informed him that Ben-Gurion and his closest advisers were waiting for him. Teddy drove Pomerantz over to Ben-Gurion's office in Jerusalem. The discussion of Eichmann's offer lasted through the night. Ben-Gurion was hopeful that some kind of deal would be worked out to save the Hungarian Jews. But the Allies refused. In the middle of a terrible war, they said, it would be a great mistake to give the Germans trucks that could help them move troops and ammunition to the battlefront. The best way to save the Jews, they said, was to win the war as quickly as possible. Ben-Gurion and the other Palestinian Jews knew by this time that no matter how quickly the war would be won it would be too late to save the Jews of Europe.

The Holocaust made clearer than ever the need for a Jewish state as a place of refuge and as a support for Jews in trouble wherever they might be.

6

Farewell to Ein Gev

Teddy turned the horse's head toward the trail heading up to the Golan Heights. Above Ein Gev, he turned to look at Lake Kinneret and at the hills of the Galilee rising to the west. It was good being back in this landscape, which he already felt to be part of him. But it was impossible to shake free from what he had seen looking through Istanbul's window into Nazi-occupied Europe. Here, above Ein Gev, the wind was the loudest thing he could hear and the world seemed to sparkle like the blue waters of the lake. It was difficult to imagine that anyone was capable of doing what the Germans were doing at that moment to the Jews in Europe. Although he himself had not set foot in the German-occupied areas, that dark corner of the world was now more real to him than Ein Gev itself. Something terrible was happening to the Jewish people, but neither he — nor anyone else, it seemed — could do anything about it.

In Palestine, the Haganah had begun to cooperate with the British in preparing for a German invasion. The German army was advancing upon Egypt, which bordered Palestine on the south. If the Germans reached Palestine, they would be met by Jewish fighters. The Jews in Europe had not been armed and had been unable to resist. The Jews in Palestine would resist. Haganah officers had drawn up plans for a last stand in the hills in the northern part of the country if the rest of the country fell.

After a few months at Ein Gev, the thirty-two-year-old kibbutznik was summoned again to Jerusalem toward the end of 1943 to resume his intelligence work. Teddy had become too valuable to the Zionist leadership to remain a farmer or fisherman. He was sent to the Egyptian capital of Cairo, just a few hours from Tel Aviv by train, to help organize the secret transfer of guns and ammunition to the Haganah. The material had been stolen from the British army. Even if the war ended with a German defeat, the Haganah knew that it would probably be fighting a war with the Arabs in the near future and it was necessary to obtain weapons if they were to survive. Teddy maintained close ties with British intelligence in Cairo and would often sit in the famous Gropi's Cafe talking with British officers.

He traveled frequently between Cairo and Jerusalem. Whenever he could, he would drive up from Jerusalem for a weekend in Ein Gev where

Tamar had remained. Usually he filled his car with British officers and journalists. He wanted not only to show them the beautiful country but also to have them meet kibbutznikim who farmed and fished, types of Jews they had never met before. Once he brought two Americans who were grandsons of President Teddy Roosevelt. After they reached Ein Gev he took them on horses up to the Golan Heights to visit an Arab village. They were treated to a large meal and traditional Arab hospitality. When they returned to the horses, however, they found that the jacket belonging to one of the Roosevelts was missing. It was a great embarrassment to the hosts, and all the villagers began looking for the missing garment. It was getting late but the Arab hosts insisted that the guests remain until they found the jacket. Fearing that it would soon be too dark to descend the Heights, Teddy came up with a solution. One of the horses, he announced, must have eaten the jacket. The villagers agreed that this must be the explanation, and Teddy and his guests were able to descend the hills to the kibbutz before darkness.

In June 1945, a few weeks after the end of the war, Teddy was sent back to England. Stopping off in Germany, he passed through some of its destroyed cities and made a detour to visit the Dachau concentration camp. Although the camp was now empty, he could feel its horror as he walked through it. The world would never be the same after this war. Certainly the Jewish people would not be the same. To Teddy, the silence of the camp where hundreds of thousands of doomed Jews had passed on their way to death was the most forceful argument that could be made for a Jewish state.

In England, he met with politicians and journalists in an attempt to win public opinion to the side of the Palestinian Jews. This was important because the British still ruled Palestine. The British government did not have much sympathy for the Jewish cause, but events were now leading them to a decision that would open the way for a Jewish state. Fighting between Arabs and Jews in Palestine was mounting, making it necessary to bring in more British troops to keep order. Once the most powerful country in the world, England had been weakened by the long war and was finding it increasingly difficult to keep troops overseas.

In addition, some 200,000 Holocaust survivors had tried to reach Palestine illegally by ships that attempted to sneak through the British blockade of the coast. Most were caught by British warships, and the refugees were placed in detention camps on the nearby island of Cyprus. This was creating strong world pressure on Britain from millions who felt the Jews had suffered enough and should not be kept in camps. These pressures finally convinced the British government that there was no alternative but to turn over responsibility for Palestine to the world community, that is, to the United Nations.

It was clear that if the British were going to leave the country a war between the Jews and the Arabs was inevitable. Returning to Palestine, Teddy spent a few months at Ein Gev but was then summoned again to work in Jewish Agency headquarters in Jerusalem. This time Tamar moved to Jerusalem with him. In the past, his long absences had led to a certain drifting apart between Tamar and Teddy. With time, however, the bond between them would prove intimate and enduring. In September 1947, Tamar gave birth in Jerusalem's Sha'are Zedek Hospital to their first child, Amos.

The following month, Teddy was summoned to David Ben-Gurion's office to receive a new assignment. To survive the expected war with the Arabs, Ben-Gurion said, the Jews in Palestine needed money and arms — lots of both and fast. The best place to get them was in the richest and most powerful country in the world, the United States. American Jews, said Ben-Gurion, were ready to help their brethren in Palestine. Two years earlier, the Haganah had established an office in New York whose mission was to obtain weapons, even if it had to be done illegally. These efforts would now have to be expanded and speeded up. Ben-Gurion asked Teddy to take over the New York operation immediately. His work would be largely secret since the United States did not permit foreigners to ship weapons out of the country without permission. The task needed someone who could think fast and deal with many types of people. Teddy accepted the assignment, the most complex and important yet given him. Saying good-bye to Tamar and their newborn son, he set off for New York to begin a new career as a gunrunner.

7

Gunrunner

Hotel Fourteen, the small hotel on New York's Upper East Side in which Teddy made his headquarters, was located above the Copacabana, the city's most famous nightclub where entertainment stars appeared every night. In the seventeen months that he spent in New York, however, there would be no more exciting show than the one Teddy himself was to direct as head of the Haganah office.

To get weapons and other supplies to Palestine two things were needed — large amounts of money and enough imagination to enable the Haganah to defy the wishes of two powerful countries. American laws forbade the shipment of war supplies from the United States, and British laws forbade their entry into Palestine. Although he always respected the law in his personal life, Teddy understood that most laws do not apply when the life of a yet unborn state was at stake. Unless he and his colleagues could fulfill their task and provide the Jews in Palestine with the means to fight, the country would be overrun by Arab armies the day the British left.

Working with a small group of Palestinian Jews and a larger group of American Jewish volunteers, he began to build an organization capable of carrying out the enormous task. It was not a very orderly organization because most of its work was secret and missions were carried out by small groups of people, or by individuals, without anyone else being told. On the one hand, Teddy had to make himself and his operation well enough known so that wealthy Jews from around the country, and even from Latin America, would give him money as a representative of the Palestinian Jews. On the other hand, if he were too well known, he would be arrested by the FBI, whose job it was to keep foreign agents — such as he was — from operating freely in the country.

A stream of visitors began coming to the Haganah office shortly after it was set up in the hotel. Sometimes a wealthy donor would walk in with a bag full of money. Sometimes it would be an arms dealer who said he had airplanes or guns to sell. Sometimes it was a scientist who said he could develop a secret weapon. Sometimes it was a man who was offering to sell a ship the Haganah could use to carry the supplies it had bought. Sometimes it was people offering to go to Palestine to help fight. Teddy met with politicians, spies, journalists, businesspeople, movie producers, junkyard owners, and bankers — anyone who could possibly help. He soon found himself also dealing indirectly with some of the toughest gangsters in America, including the Mafia. Gangsters in New York controlled the docks where ships were loaded. Bribes often had to be paid to be sure that goods would be loaded safely. Since the Haganah was shipping forbidden material, it disguised the crates. If it was sending machinery for making ammunition, for instance, it might claim that it was machinery for making stoves. Small airplanes were taken apart and put inside crates labeled prefabricated houses.

It was important that the laborers on the docks not open the crates to see what was inside or otherwise interfere with the shipments. To ensure this, Teddy sent aides to contact gang leaders. Some of the gangsters turned out to have a lot of sympathy for the idea of the Jews building their own state. This sympathy came not only from Jewish gangsters, who were then strong in New York, but from Irish and Italian gangsters as well. At one time when someone was threatening to prevent a ship from leaving, Teddy made contact with the most dangerous gang of all, known as Murder Incorporated. He did not ask the gangsters to kill anyone but their threat was enough to solve the problem. Once a disguised crate containing explosives broke open as it was being loaded on a ship and its true contents were discovered. Thanks to Teddy's connections, no one made a complaint. If someone had, the Haganah office would have been shut down and many of its employees, including Teddy, thrown into jail.

One evening, Teddy asked a young singer who had just finished performing in the Copacabana Club if he would carry a suitcase full of money to someone on the Brooklyn docks to ensure that supplies for Palestine could be loaded aboard a ship. The singer, who readily agreed, was Frank Sinatra.

Teddy discovered that he liked Americans even more than he liked the British. The Americans were more open and casual, and Teddy never had to guess about what they were really thinking. He was impressed by their politeness and basic decency.

Driven by an awareness of the life-and-death situation back home, he worked seven days a week and often went on until well after midnight. "His one relaxation was a good meal," one of his colleagues would recall years later. "Once he had that he could work twenty-four hours straight."

Late one night Teddy went with two of his assistants to consult with an ex-spy about a problem that had come up. They rang the bell of the apartment for some time, but there was no answer. Believing that the man had already gone to bed and could not hear the bell from his bedroom, Teddy left his two assistants at the door and went down to a drugstore to telephone the apartment. His call indeed woke the man, who had a phone by his bed. But when Teddy left the phone booth, he found that the drugstore had been closed, leaving him trapped inside. The owner had locked up without noticing that someone was still inside the booth. Teddy had no more coins with which to phone. He decided that there was nothing to do but spend the night there. When a guard unlocked the door two hours later to make a routine check of the store, he found a strange man sitting at the counter eating ice cream. Teddy was able to persuade the guard that he was not a thief.

Teddy expected his assistants to work as hard as he. If they went off on weekends, he would often call them back to urgent business. Once he took pity on one of them and said, "Go off for two days and don't tell me where you're staying."

Every once in a while, when they had completed some especially important mission like sending off a big shipment of guns or airplanes, he would take his staff out for a meal in a good restaurant or to a nightclub. Once he took them to a famous jazz club in Harlem. Another time he took them to a nightclub specializing in Russian music. Feeling good, Teddy rose with one of his Russian-speaking assistants to sing a Russian song in front of the audience. Teddy did not know Russian but sang what sounded to him like Russian and got a large round of applause.

Making up the rules as he went along, Teddy was operating like a magician who makes things disappear from one place — things like ships and large bombers — and appear in another place without outsiders knowing how it was done. Considerable arms were available, for instance, in France and Switzerland, but those countries would not sell them to the Palestinian Jews because England objected. To solve the problem,

Teddy flew down to Nicaragua and with the help of Jews living there obtained a meeting with the general who ruled the country. After long talks, the general agreed to purchase the arms on the Jews' behalf from the European countries. Teddy gave him several million dollars with which to make the payments. As far as the Swiss and French were concerned, the arms were being sold to Nicaragua. However, when the crates were loaded aboard ships in Europe, they were taken to Palestine instead, hidden beneath other goods in order to get them past British inspection.

The FBI was aware of what the Haganah office was trying to do, and Teddy and his team had to take precautions not to be caught in the act. They knew that the FBI was probably listening to their telephone calls and that maybe it had even placed microphones in their office. They were therefore careful about what they said and often used code words. Sometimes, when Teddy felt the FBI getting too close, he moved to another hotel. Everybody on the team was followed at some time by FBI agents, and most were called in for questioning. Teddy himself was never questioned, and he tried to avoid giving the FBI a reason to do so.

On November 27, 1947, he took time out from his work to go to the United Nations headquarters outside New York City to watch a meeting that would decide the future of the Jewish state. The United Nations was to determine on this day whether to divide Palestine between the Jews and the Arabs. The Arabs were against partition, as it was called, since they believed that all of Palestine should be an Arab state. Some countries supported the Arabs. On the other hand, many other countries believed that division of Palestine into two separate states — Jewish and Arab — was the only answer to the conflict. The tension in the United Nations hall was tremendous as the vote began. Teddy and the other Palestinian Jews present sat with scorecards to keep track of the voting. Only near the end did it become plain that Palestine would be divided. For the first time in nearly two thousand years there would be a Jewish state. Jews danced that night in Palestine and in the streets of New York.

The British were scheduled to depart from the country six months later, so the actual creation of the Jewish state would have to wait until then. By chance, Teddy was there when it happened. He had flown home in the spring of 1948 — his first visit since departing for New York — to coordinate his activities with colleagues at Haganah headquarters. Jerusalem was under siege by Arab forces, so Teddy stayed in Tel Aviv. On May 14, he made his way to the small museum in the city where Ben-Gurion was to officially announce the founding of the state. Thousands of excited people filled the street outside. Only a few hundred invited guests could fit inside the hall. Teddy had no invitation, but someone at the entrance recognized him and ushered him in. It was so crowded inside that he barely found a place to stand next to a pillar. He saw Ben-Gurion rise at a table at the front of the hall and read a short speech announcing the rebirth of a Jewish state. It would be called Israel.

Ben-Gurion's speech was broadcast on the radio. When he finished speaking, all over the country people poured into the streets and formed into circles to dance the hora. The joy was overwhelming and there was singing everywhere. All knew, however, that at that very moment Arab armies were preparing to cross the border in an attempt to eliminate the Jewish state at its moment of birth. The fight for survival was about to begin.

8

Washington Interlude

Teddy returned to New York to supervise the flow of arms to Israel, now needed more urgently than ever. He also helped recruit pilots and other war veterans, including some non-Jews, who wished to fight for the Jewish state. He followed the progress of the distant war in Israel with anxiety for the fate of the nation, his family, and his friends. Tamar and Amos had been evacuated from Ein Gev along with the other kibbutz mothers and children to the relative safety of Haifa. Teddy's parents had arrived in the country in 1939 and were living in Haifa. His brother Paul was serving with the Haganah in the north. Ein Gev, the only Jewish settlement on the eastern shore of Lake Kinneret, had taken heavy artillery shelling, and on June 10 the Syrians launched a direct assault. The attackers managed to penetrate the kibbutz at one point, but Teddy's old comrades drove them out. Attacks on the isolated settlement continued for two more days, but the kibbutznikim held their ground.

In April 1949, Teddy completed his job in New York and left for Israel after participating in a Passover seder with the other Israeli representatives in New York. The seder was also a farewell party for him. Israel had won its War of Independence, and from now on its arms purchases would be handled routinely. Teddy resumed his life as a kibbutznik and family man, once again happily stepping out of the big world to become part of a small community living on a remote lakeside in the Middle East. Ein Gev was now growing its own crops in addition to fishing, but Teddy believed that it could earn money from tourism as well. He proposed building a hotel on the shore-front south of the kibbutz. In the future, a tourist bungalow colony would indeed be built there.

Before long, Teddy's work at the kibbutz was being interrupted again by visitors and by phone calls from Jerusalem asking him to return to work for the government. A kibbutznik who heard that Teddy had declined to be ambassador to England told him he had been right to turn down the offer since he would quickly become bored by a job involving endless ceremonies and speeches. "But you're not going to remain at Ein Gev," he predicted. The kibbutznik, Zvi Brenner, who had worked with him in New York, believed that the country could not afford to let someone like Teddy Kollek disappear from public life.

Explaining his feelings years later, Brenner would say: "We were so few and we had lost so many people in the war. I felt the country would need his talents."

The prediction proved correct. After a few months Teddy accepted an offer from the Foreign Ministry to serve as the number two man in the Israeli embassy in Washington. The ambassador, Abba Eban, was also serving as ambassador to the United Nations in New York, which meant that Teddy was running the shop in Washington much of the time.

His new life in America was very different from what it had been in New York. Back then he had lived at the edge of the law, operating just one step ahead of the FBI. Now he was an official representative of his government dealing openly with American officials and living with his family. He quickly established friendly relations with many of the most important people in Washington. Some of them he had met in the Middle East during the war. One of his major tasks was to help raise money that Israel desperately needed to absorb the hundreds of thousands of immigrants pouring into the country. These included survivors of the Holocaust as well as Jews from the Arab world. Houses had to be built, and factories and farms had to be provided. The newborn country was too poor to do this on its own. Meeting with hundreds of people, Teddy played a key role in persuading Congress to provide Israel with generous assistance. He also helped raise large sums from the Jewish community.

Teddy gave high priority to establishing relations with the American intelligence community, particularly the CIA, which had been keeping its distance from Israel. The Americans, then at the beginning of the long Cold War with the Soviet Union, believed that the immigrants arriving in Israel included many Soviet spies. The mission of these spies was to learn Israel's secrets. The Americans therefore did not wish to have close ties with the Israeli intelligence community for fear that secrets shared with the Israelis would reach the Soviets.

Teddy believed that it was important to change this attitude. There were officials in Jerusalem who felt that Israel should be neutral, tying itself to neither American nor the Soviet Union. Teddy, however, believed strongly that it was in Israel's interest to become a close ally of the United States. For this it was necessary not only to persuade his Israeli colleagues but also to convince the Americans that Israel could be an important ally in the Middle East.

Searching for ways to make contact with senior American intelligence officers, Teddy approached an American Jew who had served as a colonel in army intelligence during the war. The ex-colonel said he would see what he could do. One day shortly afterward, Teddy received a phone call asking him to come to one of Washington's best-known hotels, not far from his office. Not knowing who he was going to meet, Teddy took the elevator to the floor he had been given and made his way down the carpeted hall. A tall man with a craggy face opened the door in response to Teddy's knock and ushered him in. Another man rose to shake Teddy's hand. Both of Teddy's hosts were in civilian clothing. The tall man introduced himself as a senior official of the CIA, James Angelton. The other man was an army general.

For the next few hours, Teddy attempted to explain to the two Americans that Israel was not a potential danger to American intelligence but a source of priceless information. Immigrants arriving from the Soviet Union had a lot to tell about life there. Much could be learned by putting together the thousands of pieces of information provided by these newcomers — more, probably, than America was learning from its own spies in the Soviet Union. As for the danger of Soviet spies sneaking into Israel among the immigrants, Israel was well aware of this possibility and was taking steps to deal with it. The two Americans questioned him sharply and Teddy responded openly. When the meeting finally ended, the CIA official and the general parted warmly from Teddy. This meeting would mark the beginning of a close working relationship that would prove invaluable to Israel. It would be no less useful to the Americans because of the information and other assistance Israel could provide as a strong ally in the Middle East. Teddy would retain a close personal friendship with Angelton until the latter's death some thirty years later.

After a year and a half on the job, Teddy decided that the time had come for a family vacation. He set out from Washington on a two-week car trip with Tamar and Amos. It was the longest vacation they had ever taken together. After years of ceaseless activity, Teddy decided that it was time to stop working around the clock and do something for a while that would leave him time to get to know his family. He informed his superiors that he intended to take a year's leave to study at Harvard University. However, when he returned from vacation, he found a message from Ben-Gurion waiting for him. "The old man," as everyone called Israel's first prime minister, wanted Teddy to return to Jerusalem immediately to serve as his principal assistant. Teddy was extremely upset and argued with Ben-Gurion on the telephone. He had been working around the clock for years, hadn't he? He had a family, didn't he? He was entitled to a private life, wasn't he? Reluctantly, however, he came to accept that when a prime minister asks you to serve your country you cannot say no.

Israel was already four years old when the Kolleks returned to Jerusalem. The excitement of the first years had given way to the difficult task of building a new country — creating the roads, the laws, the school system, the police, and the countless other things that go into making a nation. As director general of the prime minister's office, Teddy found himself at the very center of events. Israel's War of Independence had ended with victory, but the dangers were far from over. Prime Minister Ben-Gurion devoted his time almost entirely to Israel's relations with other countries and to strengthening the armed forces. He left other matters to his assistants. Teddy, as the chief of these assistants, was able to pick virtually anything he wanted to do. He was like a painter with a large empty canvas and lots of paint.

Wearing a tuxedo as the director general of the
prime minister's office in 1955.
(Courtesy of the Israel Government Press Office)

One of the first things he focused on was tourism.
Israel's natural beauty and its history as the Holy Land
made it a potential tourist attraction that could bring
much-needed dollars. It was, of course, the Holy Land
not just to the Jews but to Christians and Moslems as
well and therefore had deep meaning to much of the
world. But most of the historic sites still had to be
cleared of the earth that had covered them for cen-
turies. Existing sites had to be expanded and signs
posted to make them easier to visit. New hotels and
shops had to be built for tourists.

The government was so busy simply trying to provide homes and jobs for the hundreds of thousands of

Jewish refugees arriving in the country that no one was thinking seriously about tourism. Teddy, however, had always had an ability to see possibilities and turn them into realities. To develop historic sites and national parks, he got Ben-Gurion's permission to set up a special government department. He also encouraged businesspeople to invest in modern hotels. His old friend, Xiel Federmann, who had helped him smuggle out the boy from Germany in the 1930s, went to Florida at Teddy's suggestion. There he raised money from Jewish hotel owners that enabled him to start the best-known chain of hotels in Israel.

Teddy had his finger in many pies, from staying in close touch with American Jewish leaders to reorganizing radio broadcasting for Israel. The project that gave him the most pleasure, however, was the creation of Israel's first modern museum. He had inherited the love of collecting works of art from his father. But the Israel Museum in Jerusalem would not just be a place to keep pretty objects for people to look at. The museum would demonstrate that Israel was a country with a culture, not just a country with a good army. Even though it was struggling to feed and defend itself, it could still set aside the time and energy to appreciate beauty and history.

If he wished his dream of a great museum to come true, however, Teddy would have to make it happen himself. For this, the prime minister's office with all its powers was the right place to be. He began by persuading the American government to contribute a sizable sum to the museum project. He then traveled to

Presenting a birthday present to Prime Minister Levi Eshkol. (Courtesy of the Israel Government Press Office)

the United States, where he demonstrated an exceptional ability to persuade the wealthy to donate money. It was a talent that would later serve him well as mayor when he succeeded in convincing millionaires that he was doing them a favor by letting them contribute to Jerusalem. He was also able to persuade some wealthy Jews who owned great art collections to leave them in their wills to the Israel Museum. The day that the Israel Museum opened in 1965 was one of the happiest in Teddy's life. The museum would be recognized as one of the great ones in the world, and he personally had brought it into existence. So deep was his attachment to the museum that in the coming decades, no matter what other work he was doing, he would continue to maintain an office there. Even as mayor, when he was so busy that there was little time for sleep, he would retreat several hours every afternoon to his museum office. From there he continued to help raise money needed to run the rapidly growing institution.

Teddy had been with Ben-Gurion for eleven years when the prime minister decided to resign. The new prime minister, Levi Eshkol, asked Teddy to stay on, and for a year and a half he did. In January 1965, Teddy finally quit, and for the first — and only — time in his life he took a well-paying job unconnected with the government. A large real estate company in Tel Aviv asked him to serve as its president. He and his family, which now included a five-year-old daughter, Osnat, were supposed to move into Tel Aviv's fanciest suburb, where the company was building. Meanwhile, the Kolleks continued to live in Jerusalem. It was the kind of executive job Teddy's parents had wished him to end up in. But after a few months he found himself beginning to be bored. After the life he had led, selling houses was not very exciting. Nevertheless, he had no intention of returning to public life. In less than one year, however, he would be doing just that.

Ben-Gurion had gone off to live in a kibbutz in the desert; he then decided to return to politics and start his own party, called Rafi. Teddy, in an act of loyalty, supported him. On the eve of Sukkot in 1965 he and Tamar drove north from Jerusalem to spend the holiday with friends at Ein Gev. They stopped off in Tel Aviv to have lunch at the new Hilton Hotel with some of Ben-Gurion's closest supporters. These were all people with whom Teddy had worked for many years. They had a lighthearted conversation at a table overlooking the sea. When someone suggested that Teddy run for the Knesset as a member of Rafi, Teddy laughed it off. He was not the kind of person, he said, who could spend his days in a hall listening to speeches and making speeches. He was an administrator who needed to make things happen. "Then how about running for mayor of Jerusalem?" someone said. In later years, Teddy would not be certain who had first said that. The others at the table thought it was a splendid idea. Teddy's initial reaction was to dismiss it as absurd. Did they think he wanted to be in charge of collecting garbage and giving out building licenses? Jerusalem was a small town, and there was little that was as unpleasant to Teddy as small-town politics. Nevertheless, when his friends continued to press the suggestion, he said he would think about it over the holiday.

At the kibbutz, Teddy mentioned the idea to a few old friends to test their reactions. To his surprise, most were enthusiastic. For a man of action like himself the idea of sitting behind a mayor's desk had seemed a bit silly. But his friends seemed to think that it was a good idea and that he could actually make a difference in the lives of Jerusalemites. On the long drive back to Jerusalem the decision finally fell into place. He would run. He was certain that he would not win. In fact, the very thought of winning depressed him, but by running as a Rafi candidate he would be expressing his loyalty to Ben-Gurion. So unwilling was he to actually do it that Teddy did not formally register as a mayoral candidate until the very last day it was possible to do so.

Now that he was a candidate he had to have an election campaign, like it or not. To run it, he invited a bright young man named Meron Benvenisti who had worked for him in the government tourist office. In taking on the job, Meron had a very different attitude from Teddy. He did not think victory was impossible, and he intended to do all in his power to achieve it.

One of his first moves was to buy flowers on Friday afternoons. It is a custom in Israel for people to buy flowers on Friday for the Sabbath. Shops close at about 1:00 P.M. to give people time to prepare for Sabbath eve. Flowers that have not been sold by that time have little chance of being sold later. Meron and his assistants began buying large amounts of flowers after this hour for very little money. On Saturday, while everyone else rested, they attached Vote for Teddy pamphlets to every individual flower. On Saturday night, Meron and his team of young volunteers stood outside the movie houses in Jerusalem and distributed the flower messages to everyone waiting to buy a ticket. It proved an excellent way of getting Teddy's name known.

Campaigning in Jerusalem had always been a very dull affair. The candidates made a few speeches in rented halls and walked a bit through the neighborhoods shaking hands of voters. Meron hit on a new idea. Renting a small pickup truck and loudspeaker equipment, he had Teddy travel around town delivering speeches from the back of the truck. This way he could deliver several speeches a night and meet far more voters than any of the other candidates.

Teddy's feelings began to change during the campaign as he sensed himself in a real race. Toward the end, to his own surprise, he wanted to win. And win he did, by the narrowest of margins. On December 1, 1965, Teddy Kollek and his team entered City Hall. "It was like a conquering army entering a deserted city," one of his aides would recall years later. Teddy took the elevator to the top floor of the building and entered the mayor's office in the corner. Little did he imagine that he would be working there for the next twenty-eight years.

9

Mayor

The city that Teddy Kollek found himself in charge of was one of the most famous in the world. For thousands of years men had fought wars for Jerusalem and prayed for it. The direction of prayer in synagogues around the world has always been toward Jerusalem, and the Passover seder every year ends with the wish "Next year in Jerusalem." The Jews were the first to see Jerusalem as a holy city, but it became holy as well to billions of Christians and Moslems around the world.

When an Israelite army first arrived at its gates three thousand years ago, Jerusalem was already more than a thousand years old. The Israelites, as the ancient Jews are known, ruled most of the country, but here and there walled cities were still held by another people called the Canaanites. Jerusalem was one of these cities. King David wanted Jerusalem to serve as his capital because of its central location. He encircled the city and captured it. His son Solomon, when he became king, built the temple that made Jerusalem a great religious center.

For the next thousand years, the city would be the heart of the Jewish world. Its history during this period was recorded in the Bible, which would make it familiar to all the generations that followed. Jewish rule ended with the destruction of the city by the Romans in 70 C.E. Thereafter, numerous nations ruled Jerusalem. Christian armies from Europe attempted to capture Jerusalem from the Moslems in a series of wars called the Crusades. Maps produced during this period in Europe showed Jerusalem as being the center of the world.

In 1948, during Israel's War of Independence, the city once again became a battleground. Many people were killed, and for weeks the Jewish part of the city was surrounded by Arab forces and cut off from the rest of the country. The siege was finally broken, however, and when the war ended, Jerusalem was divided between Israel and Jordan.

In a sense, then, Teddy was mayor of half a city — the more modern but less interesting half. The Old City, which is located exactly where biblical Jerusalem had stood, lay on the Jordanian side of the city. It was surrounded by a wall and gates as Jerusalem had been during biblical times. Within the Old City wall lay almost all the holy places, including the Western Wall, which had been part of the ancient

Temple compound and was the holiest site in Judaism. Since the city's division in 1948, however, Jews had been unable to visit the Western Wall. Teddy would sometimes take visitors to the roof of a church on the border between the two halves of the city. This was the closest that Israelis could get to the Old City, and it was almost possible from there to see the top of the Western Wall 500 yards away.

The two halves of the city were divided by minefields and barbed wire. Streets that had once connected east and west Jerusalem were now blocked off by concrete walls. Street signs near the border had been replaced by signs warning Caution, Border Ahead". Every so often a sniper would shoot into the Jewish side of the city, but for the most part the two sides ignored each other's existence. For residents of Jerusalem there was no place on earth farther away than the other side of their own city. They could fly to Japan or South America if they wished, but they could not cross the narrow no-man's-land that separated the two Jerusalems. Occasionally, the sound of an explosion indicated that someone had tried to cross and had stepped on a mine. If he was lucky, he lost only a foot. If he was less lucky, he lost a leg or his life.

One corner of the Old City wall reached within a few yards of a Jewish neighborhood. Children playing on the streets here grew accustomed to seeing Jordanian soldiers on the ancient walls above them. Usually the soldiers ignored them. Sometimes they shouted at the children for making noise and even threw stones down at them. Sometimes there were soldiers who threw down candies.

One day an elderly nun living in a convent on the Israeli side of the border opened her mouth too wide as she leaned out of her window to look at the view and her false teeth fell out. The area into which they fell was part of no-man's-land. Only United Nations officers who were posted in Jerusalem could enter no-man's-land. Carrying a white flag to signal that they were on a peaceful mission, several United Nations officers entered as Israeli and Jordanian soldiers watched. Searching through the bushes below the convent, the officers found the false teeth, which they returned to the grateful nun.

For all the glory of its name, Jerusalem was a sleepy small town when Teddy took over. It may have been the capital of Israel, but the true heart of the country was Tel Aviv. Located atop the Judean Hills, Jerusalem took an hour and a half to reach by bus from Tel Aviv. There was little reason for anyone who was not a Jerusalemite to make the trip. With almost all the tourist sites located on the Jordanian side of the city, foreigners wishing to visit Israeli Jerusalem stayed in hotels in Tel Aviv and came up by bus for a few hours. Jerusalemites themselves had to go down to Tel Aviv if they wanted to shop for anything important, from clothing to furniture, because Jerusalem shops offered little choice. Tel Aviv was also where Jerusalemites often went for plays and concerts, since there was little cultural activity in Jerusalem. Although Jerusalem's population included families that had been living in the city for many generations, most of the residents were new immigrants from Arabic-speaking countries like Morocco and Iraq. Another large part of the Jewish population was made up of ultra-religious Jews dressed in black who lived in a world of their own, a world of study and prayer. But Jerusalem was also the nation's capital and home of The Hebrew University, the biggest university in the country. The pleasant, tree-lined neighborhood of Rehavia, where Teddy lived, was home to many university professors and government ministers.

There was virtually no nightlife in the city. After cinemas emptied at 11:00 P.M. the few cafés still open closed up and the streets emptied. Israel did not yet have television, and people lived quiet lives at home.

Searching for ways to build up a nightlife that might draw tourists overnight, Teddy decided to begin by lighting up the Israel Museum from the outside at night. It would at least provide something to look at. He soon discovered, however, that there was not enough money to light it more than two nights a week.

City Hall, where Teddy had his office, was located on the border between the two halves of the city. Its walls were chipped by many bullet holes from the War of Independence, and it was still an easy target for Jordanian soldiers. Shortly after taking over, Teddy discovered that there were plans to build a new City Hall in a safer area away from the border. He ordered that the plans be scrapped. Many of the new immigrants, he pointed out, were living along the border. It would be a bad example for the city's leaders to move

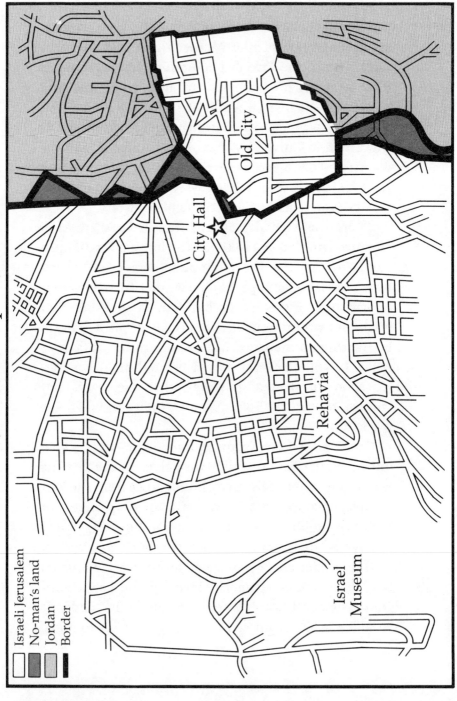

Divided Jerusalem, pre-June, 1967

Israeli Jerusalem
No-man's land
Jordan
Border

Old City

City Hall

Rehavia

Israel Museum

Before the Six-Day War, Jerusalem's City Hall was located almost on the border of the divided city.

to safety while leaving the poor living along the dangerous border with nowhere else to go. In addition, he said, the city would one day be reunited, and when that happened, the existing City Hall would once again be at its center. That prediction seemed unreal to the people who heard it, and even Teddy never imagined that it would be fulfilled while he was still in the mayor's office.

Meanwhile, the enthusiasm with which he had begun his job soon began to fade. Supporters of the different political parties were constantly making deals

With Rabbi Menahem Porush, head of one of the religious parties on Jerusalem's city council. (Courtesy of the Israel Government Press Office)

with each other and against each other. All his life Teddy had been involved in making people work together for a common goal and he had no patience for politics. In addition, the nature of the work proved boring. For someone who had spent years as a secret agent, a gunrunner, and head of the prime minister's office there was little challenge in dealing with questions like whether or not to permit someone to add another floor to his house or enclose a balcony. He had been elected to a four-year term, but by the end of one year he had begun to wonder whether he would be able to stay on the job for another three. The question would disappear on the morning of June 5, 1967, in a puff of smoke, the smoke that covered Jerusalem with the opening barrage of the Six-Day War.

10

A United Jerusalem

The general with the black eye patch sitting across the table from Teddy, Defense Minister Moshe Dayan, was the hero of the Six-Day War, which had ended just three weeks before. From the terrace of the King David Hotel overlooking the Old City, they could see and hear some of the results of Israel's spectacular victory — bulldozers clearing no-man's-land of barbed wire, soldiers clearing minefields. The army was still in control of the captured Arab part of Jerusalem, and civilians were not permitted to cross over into what had been for so long enemy territory.

In addition to Teddy, key officials, including the chief of police, had come to discuss with Dayan the future of the city in the wake of the Knesset's decision to unite the two halves of Jerusalem. Dayan kept the discussion short. Tomorrow, June 29, the border would be opened to everyone, said Dayan. Jews would be able to freely visit the Old City, and Arabs would be able to visit the Jewish side of the city.

His listeners, including Teddy, were stunned. Too soon, they said. How could two peoples who had been enemies so long be expected to become peaceful neighbors overnight? There would be a massacre, they warned. Arabs would kill Jews. Jews would kill Arabs. Time had to pass before the two peoples could be permitted to mix.

General Dayan let everyone speak and then repeated what he had said. "The government has decided that the two parts of Jerusalem are to be united. It isn't a united city if all its residents can't move freely in it. From tomorrow morning this is one city and that means no border."

Shortly after dawn the next day the concrete walls and barbed-wire barriers still dividing Jerusalem were removed and civilians began to cross. Only a few went at first but then more and more. Arabs and Jews examined each other with curiosity as they passed at the crossing points. By midday Jerusalem looked as if it was celebrating an enormous festival as Arab and Jewish residents crossed in massive numbers to see the half of the city so long forbidden to them. Older Jerusalemites, Jews and Arabs who had been friends before the city's division in 1948, found each other and embraced. Tensions between Arabs and Jews would reemerge soon enough, but on this day there was only wonder that what had so long been impossible was now possible.

Teddy hitching a ride.
(Courtesy of the Israel Government Press Office)

The world had changed for all Jerusalemites but for no one as much as for Teddy Kollek. The city that he was now mayor of was three times the size of the city he had been mayor of the day before. And many times more complicated. No mayor in the world faced the range of problems that now confronted him. Jerusalem was no longer a sleepy border town. It was a world in itself, one full of tensions and potential conflict. Teddy had had many challenging jobs in the past but none as challenging as this. All that he had done in his life was preparation for what now awaited him. All thoughts he had had of leaving the job and becoming a business executive again were forgotten.

Like Franz Josef, the emperor of his childhood, Teddy presided over a population of many nationalities. The Jewish population itself came from more than eighty countries. There were Jews from the Caucasus Mountains in Russia and the Atlas Mountains in Morocco, from Budapest and Buenos Aires, from America and Afghanistan. They were all Israelis now, but they maintained their own traditions. Many prayed in their own synagogues and at home spoke the language of the country in which they had been born. The Jewish population was divided into two main groups — Sephardim, who originated mostly in Arabic-speaking countries, and Ashkenazim, who originated in Europe.

Jerusalem's unification had added Arabs to this mixture. They now made up more than a quarter of the city's population. The annexation of the Old City with its numerous churches also brought the concern of Christians around the world about what was happening in Jerusalem.

To run a city inhabited by so many different groups, often quareling with each other, a mayor had to be like a kindergarten teacher constantly trying to keep the children from pushing each other in the sandbox. He also had to find the time to take each child aside to hear his problems and make him feel good about himself.

The mayor's car stopped in the center of the Arab neighborhood where a group of local residents was waiting to receive him. Some wore *kheffiyas,* or Arab headdresses. Most were dressed in suits in honor of their distinguished visitor. Teddy was led into a large house where chairs had been set up in a circle in the living room. On the walls were inscriptions from the Koran, the Moslem holy book. The *mukhtar,* or headman, of the village rose to his feet. Every Arab neighborhood had a *mukhtar* who represented the community. Although most Arabs in Jerusalem learned to speak good Hebrew, the elderly *mukhtar* had asked a young man from the village to translate for him.

Everyone had heard of Mayor Teddy, began the *mukhtar,* and everyone had great respect for him. "He has done much for our neighborhood already but problems remain." There was, for instance, an open drainage ditch that carried rainwater pouring down from the hillside above. "The current is strong enough to sweep away a camel," said the *mukhtar.* Unless it was covered, there was danger that a child might be drowned.

As Teddy smoked a cigar, the *mukhtar* completed his list of requests and was followed by another resident who recited a list of his own, including the need for new bulbs for the street lamps. Other men in the room mentioned the need for repairing the main road and permits to build new homes. Sometimes they addressed their guest as Mr. Mayor, sometimes Teddy. After sipping delicious coffee served in small porcelain cups, Teddy told his hosts that he would be able to fulfill some of their requests but not all. The city simply did not have enough money to meet all the needs of its citizens. But whatever could be done would be done. When he left, he was given a warm farewell.

Teddy made such visits to Arab and Jewish neighborhoods several times a week. For him it was the best way to keep track of the mood of the city. "In running a city you have to understand what people want," he said. The residents themselves were left with a sense that someone cared about them — someone no less than the city's mayor. Teddy made special efforts to meet the needs of the Arab population. Their defeat in the war had left them with a sense of humiliation and bitterness. Teddy did not expect them to welcome being ruled by Israel, but he nevertheless wanted them to feel at home in the city in which they had been living for more than a thousand years. He did not want them to feel like a conquered people. He persuaded the government to drop its plans to introduce an Israeli study program into Arab schools in the city instead of the Jordanian curriculum they had been following. Most of the Arab students, he argued, would want to go to universities in the Arab world and therefore needed an acceptable high school diploma. An Israeli diploma would be of no use in the Arab world. Even if Jordan was an enemy country, he said, the city's Arab students should be permitted to continue using its textbooks and taking its examinations. The Israeli government finally agreed.

Some of the Arab merchants refused to have store

signs in Hebrew in addition to their Arabic signs as required by Israeli law. Teddy chose not to fine the merchants. "If there's a sign on a bakery in Arabic and there is no Hebrew sign, whom would it hurt?" he asked. "We want to prevent unnecessary friction."

On the anniversary of the Six-Day War, Jewish residents would place flowers on memorials for the Israeli soldiers killed in the battle for the city in 1967. Arab leaders requested to put up a memorial as well on their side of the city for Arab soldiers killed in the war. There was an angry debate in the City Council over the matter. It was unthinkable, said some councilmen, to permit a memorial to be put up for soldiers who had fought against Israel, especially in a war that the Arabs had started. Teddy, however, favored the idea and most members of the council supported him. The Arabs of East Jerusalem were citizens of the city, he said. "They mourn their dead the way we mourn our dead." When the army wanted to stage a military parade that would pass through the Arab part of the city, Teddy persuaded it to change the route so as not to humiliate the Arab residents.

Mordecai Darwish entered the synagogue as Saturday prayers started at 6:30 A.M.. The city's chief gardener, Darwish had been given a highly unusual assignment by the mayor. After the reading of the Torah, the rabbi rose to address the congregation. "We have with us today a guest from City Hall who would like to talk briefly to you. Please give him your attention."

Darwish took the podium to deliver a sermon he had grown accustomed to making. For months, he had been attending Sabbath services at Teddy's request in the poorest parts of the city. These neighborhoods had almost no trees or flowers and Teddy was determined to provide some greenery to the drab streets. Every time the city gardeners finished their work, however, neighborhood children uprooted the young trees and plants as a prank. The residents were mostly from poor areas in North Africa and Iraq that had likewise been without greenery, so trees or flowers were not things missing from their lives. When children pulled up the roots, therefore, the adults were not upset. Teddy, however, insisted that the gardeners return and plant again. "Otherwise we won't have any trees left in the city," he said.

Darwish told the congregation that their neighborhood could be as pleasant as wealthier parts of the city. For this it needed trees and grassy parks and flower beds. It was essential, said Darwish, for the adults to explain to the children that trees belonged to the neighborhood itself.

From this synagogue, Darwish proceeded to another where prayers had started an hour later. Here too, with the rabbi's permission, he delivered his sermon. His preaching was not confined to synagogues. During the week he visited schools to talk to student assemblies. Walking down streets where plantings had been carried out, he would stop to chat with shop owners and street vendors. "Would you please keep an eye out and make sure the kids don't harm the trees?" In the

Teddy with his brother Paul (left) and Mordecai Darwish, the chief municipal gardener.
(Courtesy of Teddy Kollek)

parks, he would stop to talk to groups of youngsters, passing out chewing gum and candies as he spoke to them about the pride they would take in their neighborhood when the trees grew.

Slowly, his message took hold. On one street, a flower bed was uprooted five times. The sixth time it remained untouched. On another street a young tree was uprooted and its replacement died when youths peeled off its bark. The third tree, however, took root. Under Teddy's direction, the city's appearance was transformed as tens of thousands of trees and hundreds of thousands of flowers were planted. "When the city began planting trees here a few years ago," said a woman in one of the poorer neighborhoods years later, "they seemed strange objects to the kids who pulled them down. But to the youngsters growing up nowadays the trees and flowers all around them have become part of their lives and it would seem strange without them."

It would take more than trees, however, to improve the lives of the city's residents. Imagination was needed and money, lots of money. Teddy believed that a city must be more than just a collection of houses and streets. Jerusalem was too poor a city to afford much beyond necessities like garbage collection and street repairs. Its residents — mostly new immigrants and the ultra-religious — were far poorer than Tel Aviv residents and paid little in taxes. The national government too had little money to spare. But no one in Israel had a greater ability to raise money from the wealthy than Teddy himself. Flying abroad frequently on fund-raising trips, he would, over time, receive hundreds of millions of dollars in donations, a tremendous amount. He used the money to build modern community centers all over the city as well as new public libraries and parks. Money went, too, for modern theaters and concert halls. Critics at first said that these facilities were too grand for a city like Jerusalem and that they would remain empty. Almost from the start, however, they were filled with residents hungry for culture. At Teddy's suggestion, elementary school students were taken to a play at least once a year to familiarize them with the theater.

Nor were sports fans neglected. Two small, sad-looking soccer fields that had served Jerusalem for years were replaced with a modern soccer stadium. Despite Teddy's objections, the donor insisted as a condition for giving the money that it be called Teddy Stadium.

The old building called Mishkenot Sha'ananim (peaceful dwellings) across the valley from the Old City walls was a slum when Teddy first saw it, but he felt that it deserved a better fate. Dating from 1860, Mishkenot was the first residence built outside the ancient walls. Until then, the entire population had crowded into the walled Old City for fear of the bandits who roamed the country. Every night the gates of the city were shut to prevent bandits from entering.

A wealthy British Jew, Sir Moses Montefiore, often visited the country to help its small Jewish population. He was appalled at the crowded and unsanitary conditions inside Jerusalem's Jewish Quarter. He urged the Jews to begin building new quarters outside the walls where there was space and sunlight. The security situation was improving, and if there was still danger from bandits outside the walls, there was greater danger from disease inside.

To encourage the Jews to move out, he built Mishkenot on a hill opposite the Old City. The long one-story building was divided into sixteen apartments. At each end was a synagogue, one Ashkenazic and one Sephardic. Sir Moses announced that no rent would be charged. It was a tempting offer but there was such great fear of living outside the walls that few accepted it. The first families that dared to move in spent only the daylight hours there initially, returning before dark to sleep inside the walls. As time passed and they felt safer, they began to stay through the night. Sir Moses constructed a windmill near Mishkenot so that those living in the area could work grinding flour from the wheat brought by farmers. Within a few years other Jews began to build neighborhoods outside the walls as well.

Almost a century later, Mishkenot was to become a dangerous place again. With the division of the city in 1948 between Israel and Jordan, the structure was in view of Jordanian soldiers on the Old City walls and there was occasional sniping. The only people living in Mishkenot were those too poor to live anywhere else. After the Six-Day War, Teddy decided to turn the historic old building into a special kind of guest house. Jerusalem was far from the centers of world culture, but this could be offset in part, he believed, by bringing to the city top writers, artists, and scholars from abroad. They would spend a few days or weeks at Mishkenot and exchange ideas with Israeli colleagues and perhaps with the public as well. Teddy persuaded an American businessman to put up the money to turn the old building into a beautiful apartment complex. Over the years its distinguished guests would greatly enrich Jerusalem's cultural life.

The atmosphere in the courtyard of the old Turkish inn that had been converted to a theater was like that aboard a cruise ship on its first night at sea. Strangers stood with drinks in their hands looking about them for people to talk to. Many of the faces they saw were well known to them from newspapers and magazines. There were famous architects and town planners and scholars from all over the world. They had been invited by Teddy in 1969 to the first meeting of the Jerusalem Committee.

When the guests took their seats, Teddy explained why he had asked them to come to Jerusalem. Although the Israeli flag flew over Jerusalem, he said, the city did not belong only to Israel. The entire world had an interest in Jerusalem; therefore, he wanted to

Teddy addressing visitors in the two-thousand-year-old Citadel
in the Old City.
(Courtesy of the Israel Government Press Office)

give the world a say in how it was developed. "All of us have two hometowns," one of the guests agreed, "the city we live in and Jerusalem." In meetings over the coming years, the experts would advise Teddy about roads, tall buildings, and other planning aspects. Beyond the value of the advice itself, the committee was Teddy's answer to demands abroad that Jerusalem be made an international city run by the United Nations. Jerusalem was too important, said those who supported this idea, to be left in the hands of one religion. The Jerusalem Committee showed that Israel respected the opinions of the world community and had no wish to turn Jerusalem into just a Jewish city.

Few cities in the world had a more mixed population than Jerusalem. Teddy wanted to keep it that way. The United States celebrated "the melting pot" in which immigrants from many nations became Americans sharing the same culture. The tradition of the Middle East, however, was not that of the melting pot but of the "mosaic" in which each group retained its specific identity. With Teddy's help, museum exhibitions were mounted about different ethnic groups to encourage these groups to have pride in themselves. The ethnic communities were also helped to revive customs they had followed in their countries of origin. Jews in Morocco, for example, had marked the day after Passover with picnics and home visits, a cheerful day of celebration they called Maimouna. In Israel they discovered that other Jews did not celebrate the day and for the most part they abandoned it. With

Teddy's encouragement, the Moroccan Jews in Jerusalem revived it. The first year only some three hundred participated in the celebrations. Within a few years, tens of thousands of people were participating, and the custom had spread all over the country. "You've got to give people pride in what they are," said Teddy. "This makes them more secure."

As for the attitude of Jerusalem's Arabs toward Israel, this would not easily change, Teddy acknowledged. "They will continue to regard their culture as threatened by our way of life. But when people ask, 'When will there be integration?' or 'Why don't the Jews and Arabs love each other?' they have an absolutely wrong concept of what can be achieved. The Jews and Arabs will not easily love each other in this generation or the next and it isn't necessary. The question is whether we can find a way to live together. This is a matter for generations. We have no choice but to carry on."

11

The Last Race

Teddy glanced at the clock next to his bed as he reached for the ringing phone. It was two o'clock in the morning.

"There are workers fixing a pipe on the street outside my house," said the caller. "They're drilling and it's impossible to sleep."

"Why are you calling me?" asked Teddy sleepily.

"Because you're the mayor, and if I can't sleep, then neither will you."

Teddy was one of the few mayors in the world who kept his number listed in the phone book. It was important, he felt, that the public know that if all else failed there was someone they could turn to. Not even nuisance phone calls would change his mind.

Mostly it was his ever-patient wife, Tamar, who took the calls because Teddy arrived home late almost

Teddy, near the Western Wall, with his driver, Nahum, behind him at left.
(Courtesy of the Israel Government Press Office)

every night. For many years his young driver, Nahum, tried to keep up with him, but it finally became too exhausting. A second driver had to be hired to take Teddy around to his appointments at night. These included neighborhood meetings, speeches, and dinners with people who might contribute something to the city. Teddy made up for missing sleep by napping during the day, often at public events. He regularly dozed off on public platforms in full view of the audience as speeches were being made. His own speeches usually lasted for no more than a minute or two.

Teddy was the first person at City Hall almost every morning, arriving by 6:30 A.M.. After a few

Teddy caught napping at one of the many public events that he attended as mayor.
(Courtesy of the Israel Government Press Office)

moments spent at his desk to see what meetings were scheduled for the day, he would join Nahum in the car. For the next hour they would tour neighborhoods to see what needed doing. Removing a pad from his jacket pocket, Teddy made notes about what he saw— a streetlight that wasn't working, pedestrian crossings that needed repainting, a street that needed more trees, garbage that had not been collected. When he returned to his office, his secretary was already waiting and he would drop the pad on her desk. She typed

Behind his desk in City Hall, 1990.
(Courtesy of the Israel Government Press Office)

up his notes and sent messages to heads of the depart-
ments to fix the things Teddy had noted. Within a few
days, he would make a point of driving back to see
whether the corrections had been carried out. If they
had not been, Teddy would be on the phone with some
hard words for the department head.

Such attention to detail marked everything he did.
At the opening of a large archaeological site to the
public, he took one of his assistants aside to ask what
arrangements had been made to water the one tree in
the area. From his tone of concern one might have
thought it was the only tree left in the city. Riding

with Nahum near the Israel Museum one day, he suddenly shouted at him to stop the car. A tourist was picking a flower from one of the flower beds on the side of the road. As Teddy jumped out of the car and ran toward her, the woman looked up startled.

"What do you think you're doing?" he shouted.

"Just picking a flower," she said. The woman spoke English in an American accent and it was plain that she did not know who this wild-looking man shouting at her was.

"Would you do this in your hometown?" he asked.

"It's just one flower."

"Do you know what would happen if every tourist picked just one flower?" he answered.

When this story was printed in a newspaper, another tourist sent Teddy a hundred-dollar bill. "Flowers apparently are worth a lot to you," he wrote. "This is to pay for the one that was picked."

Attention to detail, however, did not just mean getting angry at people when they did something wrong. Since his youth he had made a point of remembering people's birthdays and sending cards or gifts. Even as a busy mayor he would find time to dash off handwritten notes of congratulations on happy occasions and notes of appreciation for work well done. An American immigrant woman whose windows had been hit repeatedly by stones thrown by Arab youths was surprised one day to see Jerusalem's mayor standing in her doorway. With him was Tamar. They had seen the woman interviewed on television and had come to express their support. Teddy did not forget to bring a box of candy.

Teddy and Tamar in 1974.
(Courtesy of Teddy Kollek)

His enthusiasm for his work was matched by a sharp temper felt by workers who failed to carry out their duties. Nor did he hesitate to take a punch at citizens from time to time when they got him sufficiently upset. "I don't think everybody should be permitted to insult public officials," he said after slapping a twenty-seven-year-old man he thought had insulted him. Once he got so angry at a group of women who came to his office to shout at him that he offered to fight the one man who had accompanied them. "I may be old but I can still knock your teeth out," said the mayor, then sixty-five. The man, less than half Teddy's age, hurriedly backed away. Surprisingly, these incidents never damaged his popularity. They seemed, indeed, to add to his reputation as "a real person" who behaved not the way politicians were supposed to behave but the way he really felt.

This ability to have people believe in him had been a key to his success since he was a youth leader in Vienna. Even strangers felt immediately that the Teddy they met was the real Teddy, not someone whose true nature they would discover only later. The wealthy people whom he approached for money gave it so readily because they sensed that he really believed in what he was doing and that they could trust him to use the money well. Poor people in Jerusalem voted for him even though he was from a different party than the one they usually voted for. They did so because they felt that he cared about them and was not just trying to get their votes.

Being honest did not mean being stuffy. Teddy had a sense of humor that always enlivened meetings. He also had a sense of fun. He never hesitated to put on a firefighters' helmet, pose as a shoe-shine boy, or assume some other role that might cheer things up. He addressed numerous groups every week—from Moroccan Jews and ultra-Orthodox Jews to Arabs, Christian clergy, and visiting scholars. He was always able to find the right thing to say.

The friends he made over the years included many celebrities. Teddy was particularly friendly with the comedian Danny Kaye, a master chef who would cook for him whenever Teddy came to Los Angeles. Good food was something Teddy found hard to resist. Chubby as he was and already close to sixty-five, he cheerfully put on shorts and a T-shirt to join the City Hall soccer team in a game against a team of government workers.

Teddy was friendly with many of the world's leading scholars and politicians and would often visit them when he was abroad. His closest friend, however, remained the woman he had married. He and Tamar would take breakfast together at 5:30 A.M. every morning, and it was in those quiet moments that Teddy was able to express his deepest feelings and raise the most troubling questions. Tamar, a shy woman devoted to Teddy and their family, always avoided the public light. But Teddy relied on her common sense and on her evaluation of people and situations more than he relied on anyone else's. "Never for a moment have we missed the comforts of Vienna," she said in a rare interview as she recalled how both she and Teddy had suffered from serious diseases at Kibbutz Ein Gev and lived in very hard conditions. "We came with certain expectations, and happily all those dreams were fulfilled."

In 1993, Teddy was completing his twenty-eighth year as mayor and was looking forward to finally stepping down. He was already eighty-two years old and his health was no longer what it used to be. Although his workday began an hour or so later than it used to, he was still seldom home before midnight. The time had come to enjoy grandchildren and the other quiet pleasures of life.

Teddy in his last year as Jerusalem's mayor.
(Courtesy of the Israel Government Press Office)

The Labor Party to which he belonged, however, asked him to run again. Just one more time. Peace negotiations had begun and the future of Jerusalem might be decided in the coming few years. It was important, said the party leaders, to have Teddy as mayor at this critical time. Everything he had built up in Jerusalem was at stake. It was an argument that Teddy found difficult to reject. All his life he had done what had to be done regardless of his own comfort. He decided that he could not abandon Jerusalem now.

The campaign for mayor was a strange one. The candidate running against Teddy did not have a bad word to say about him. On the contrary, he admitted that Teddy was a great man who had done great things for Jerusalem. He pointed to only one problem—Teddy's age. If Teddy won the election and served the five-year term, he would be eighty-seven when he finished. Could someone this age really do the job?

It was a reasonable question, but nevertheless most experts believed that Teddy would win again. How could Jerusalem vote against Teddy Kollek? The question about age, however, was one that many Jerusalemites who had supported Teddy in the six previous elections were now asking themselves. Reporters interviewing people in the streets heard the same remark very often—"He's done wonderful things, but he's too old for the job now."

On election night, Teddy was in his car when the results were broadcast on the radio. The announcer sounded unbelieving as he said that Teddy Kollek, running for reelection as Jerusalem's mayor, had lost. Forgetting the need to be neutral in reporting election results, the announcer could not help referring to Teddy's loss as "a tragedy." Although Teddy had half expected it, he could not help but feel the blow. As with his first election twenty-eight years before, he had not wanted to run at the beginning, but once he entered the race he was in it to win. Teddy asked Nahum to drive him home and wait in the car. He went up for a few moments to his third-floor apartment to share the news with Tamar. When he returned to the car, he seemed calm. Nahum drove him to campaign headquarters, where the volunteers who had worked so hard for his reelection had gathered. Everyone applauded when Teddy entered but the mood was dismal. Some volunteers were crying.

Teddy stood silently for a moment, looking thoughtful rather than sad. "I served the city before I was mayor," he said, referring to his founding of the Israel Museum. "I will find a way to continue serving the city."

The last stop before going home was the Jerusalem Theatre, where a dinner was being given in Teddy's honor. The guests were mostly wealthy people from abroad who over the years had provided Teddy with the money he had used to rebuild Jerusalem. They had come to celebrate what they had expected to be his last victory.

No performance was being given in the theater that night, so the tables for the dinner had been set up onstage. Between courses, singers entertained the guests. The dinner had begun in Teddy's absence. As he approached the stage from the wings, he could hear a woman singing a familiar song. Twenty-six years before, on the eve of the Six-Day War, a song contest had been held in Jerusalem with the participation of the country's top singers. Teddy, who had been mayor little more than a year, asked one of the best songwriters in the country, Naomi Shemer, to write one about Jerusalem. Her song, "Jerusalem of Gold," would become one of the most popular the country had ever known. Its beautiful words and melody reflected the special place Jerusalem had in the hearts of the Jewish people and the sadness that Jews could no longer reach the Old City. Two weeks later Israeli soldiers captured the Old City, and the songwriter changed the words to reflect the joy at this return. Whenever "Jerusalem of Gold" was played in the years afterward, it would raise memories of those days that so dramatically changed the life of the nation.

When Teddy emerged onstage, it took a moment for his eyes to adjust to the darkness. All the lights had been turned off except for one thin spotlight shining directly down on the singer. The tables at which the guests sat were dimly reflected in the light. As Teddy stood listening to the song that he had caused to be written, in the theater that he had built, surrounded by people whose money he had used to change the face of Jerusalem, it was as if his twenty-eight years as mayor had come together in the very hour that his role in the city was coming to an end.

Someone saw Teddy standing silently in the darkness. A spotlight suddenly flashed on, and he was caught in a beam like the one enveloping the singer across the stage. There was a rustle as people turned to look and then a burst of applause as the guests recognized the familiar figure standing in the light. The singer smiled at Teddy and nodded as he joined her in singing the final stanza of "Jerusalem of Gold."

IMPORTANT DATES
IN THE LIFE OF TEDDY KOLLEK

1911   Teddy Kollek is born on May 27 in Nagyvaszony, a
       village overlooking the Danube River near
       Budapest, in the Austro-Hungarian Empire.

1918   Settles with his family in Vienna, Austria, after
       the end of the First World War.

1922   Joins a Zionist club.

1924   Celebrates his bar mitzvah in the main synagogue
       in Vienna.

1930   Prepares for a pioneering life at a training farm in
       Austria.

1934   Rescues a Jewish child from the hands of the
       Gestapo in Germany.

1935   Arrives in Palestine as a pioneer and helps found
       Kibbutz Ein Gev.

1937   Marries Tamar.

1938   Sent on a mission to Europe to train young people preparing for emigration to Palestine; obtains exit permits for young Jews from Nazi-occupied areas.

1941   Returns to England to aid in the Zionist movement; meets Ben-Gurion and Weizmann in war-torn London.

1943   Operates as a secret agent in Istanbul, Turkey, joining other Palestinian Jewish agents to make contact with Jews remaining in Europe.

1947   Tamar gives birth to the Kolleks' first child, Amos, in September. The following month Teddy is sent by Ben-Gurion to New York to head the Haganah's underground gunrunning operation.

1948   The State of Israel is declared, and Teddy attends the formal ceremony in Tel Aviv.

1951   Serves as the number two man at the Israeli embassy in Washington.

1952   Returns to Israel, where he is appointed director general of the Prime Minister's office in Jerusalem.

1960   The Kolleks' daughter, Osnat, is born.

1965   Elected mayor of Jerusalem.

1993   Defeated in his bid for reelection after twenty-eight years as Jerusalem's mayor.

Index

Note: Page numbers in italics indicate photographs.

Angelton, James, 73
Anti-Semitism, 11, 13, 20, 26
Arabs
   attitude of, toward Israel,
      105
   British government and, 47
   Haganah and, 45–46
   and partitioning of Palestine,
      66–67
   relations of, with Teddy,
      36, 57, 95–97, 105
   after reunification of
      Jerusalem, 92, 94
   threat of war from, 59, 62
   in War of Independence,
      68, 84
Austria-Hungary,
   after First World War, 10

Ben-Gurion, David, *46*
   announces creation of Israel,
      67–68
   asks Teddy to be gunrunner,
      59
   and Eichmann's offer to
      save Jews, 53, 54
   as head of Jewish Agency, 44
   as leader of Zionist
      movement, 42–43
   names Teddy his principal
      assistant, 74
   resigns as prime minister, 78
   starts Rafi party, 78
Benvenisti, Meron, 80–81
Brand, Yoel, 52
Brenner, Zvi, 70–71
British government

relinquishes Palestine to
United Nations, 58
as ruler of Palestine, 44–45,
47, 58

City Hall, in Jerusalem, 33, 87,
89
Concentration camps, 50, 52,
57–58

Dafni, Reuven, 27, 28, 32, 34
Darwish, Mordecai, 97–99, 99
Dayan, Moshe, 91–92

Eban, Abba, 71
Egypt, in Six-Day War, 2
Eichmann, Adolf, 40, 41, 52, 53
Ein Gev. See Kibbutz Ein Gev
Eshkol, Levi, 77, 78

Federmann, Xiel, 22–23, 76
Fogel, Yossi, 35
Franz Josef, 10, 94
Freud, Sigmund, 12

Gestapo, 22, 23

Haganah
under FBI suspicion, 66
obtains weapons for
Palestine, 59, 61, 62, 63
Paul Kollek serves in, 69
prepares for German invasion
of Palestine, 56
prepares for war with Arabs,
45
Herzl, Theodor, 12
Hitler, Adolf, 20, 21
Holocaust, 26, 50–51, 54, 58
Hungary, Jews in, 52

Israel. See also Palestine
creation of, 46, 67

tourism in, 70, 75–76
Israel Museum, 76–78, 87
Istanbul, Turkey, 48–52

Jerusalem
as divided city, 3, 84, 85
history of, 83–84
Old City of, 84–85
population of, 86–87
reunited, by Six-Day War,
5, 91–92
Jerusalem Committee, 103–104
"Jerusalem of Gold," 117–118
Jewish Agency, 44–46, 59
Jews
American, and Zionism, 43,
59, 62
in concentration camps, 50,
52, 57–58
discrimination against, 11,
13, 20, 26
in Vienna, 11–12, 13
Jordan, 2, 3

Kibbutz Ein Gev
early years of, 30–37
Syrian assault on, 69–70
Teddy's return to, 41, 44
tourist colony on, 70
Kibbutzim, 17–18
Kollek, Alfred (Teddy's father),
7, 8, 9, 13, 39, 69
Kollek, Amos (Teddy's son),
59, 69
Kollek, Emil (Teddy's uncle), 9
Kollek, Osnat (Teddy's daughter),
78
Kollek, Paul (Teddy's brother),
7, 17, 39, 69, 99
Kollek, Rachel (Teddy's mother),
8–9, 10, 12–13, 39, 69
Kollek, Tamar (Teddy's wife),
28, 35, 41, 107

evacuated from Ein Gev, 69
gives birth to Amos, 59
marries Teddy, 34
meets Teddy, 26
photos of, *27, >112*
relationship of, with Teddy,
   59, 114
Kollek, Teddy
   arrives in Palestine as
      pioneer, 29
   attends ceremony declaring
      State of Israel, 67
   bar mitzvah of, 14–15
   birth of, 7
   children of, 59, 78
   CIA and, 72–73
   decides to study at
      Harvard University, 74
   as director general of prime
      minister's office, 74–78, *75*
   elected mayor of Jerusalem,
      81
   finishes high school, 19
   First World War and, 9–10
   founds Israel Museum 76–78
   at Franz Josef's funeral, 10
   friendships of, 113–114
   as fund-raiser for Israel, 71,
      100–101
   as gunrunner, 59–66, 69
   as intelligence officer,
      46–54, 56
   as Israeli embassy official,
      71–73
   in Istanbul, 48–52
   Jewish Agency and, 44–46, 59
   Jewish home life of, 12–13
   at Kibbutz Ein Gev, 30–37,
      41, 44, 70, 79
   loses mayoral election,
      116–118
   marries Tamar, 34
   as mayor of Jerusalem

   cultural projects of,
      102–105
   of divided city, 84–90
   fund-raising of,
      100–101
   gardening projects
      under,97–99
   relations with Arabs,
      36, 57, 94–97, 105
   after reunification of
      city 91–105
   work habits of,
      108–111
   meets British intelligence
      agents, 44
   meets Chaim Weizmann, 43
   meets David Ben-Gurion,
      42
   meets Tamar, 26
   moves to Berlin, 9
   moves to Vienna, 10
   named after Theodor Herzl, 12
   obtains exit permits from
      Eichmann, 41
   parents' hopes for, 19, 20
   pastimes of, 15
   personality traits of, 113
   photos of, *31, 46, 75,*
      77, 89, 93, 99, 103, 108,
      109, 110, 112, 115
   as poor student, 8
   promotes tourism in Israel,
      70, 75–76
   quits high school, 18
   as real estate company
      president, 78
   relationships of
      with parents, 8
      with Tamar, 59, 114
   rescues Jewish child from
      Gestapo, 21–25
   runs for mayor of
      Jerusalem, 79–81

in Six-Day War, 1–5
sleep habits of, 27–28, 108,
    109
temper of, 112–113
on training farm in
    Palestine, 18–19
trains emigrants for
    Palestine, 39–40
in Zionist movement
        in Czechoslovakia,
            19–20, 21–22, 25
        in England, 28, 39, 40,
            41–44, 58
        in Germany, 20–21
        in New York, 59–67,
            69, 70
        in Palestine, 18–19
        in Romania, 25
        in Vienna, 13–14, 16,
            18, 40–41

Mishkenot Sha'anamin,
    101–102
Montefiore, Moses, 101–102

Nagyvaszony, as Teddy's
    birthplace, 7
Nahum, 108, *108*, 109, 111, 116
Nazis, 20, 21, 26, 39, 40

Old City (Jerusalem), 84–85,
    94, 101, 102

Palestine. *See also* Israel
    American aid to, 59, 61–62
    British declaration
        supporting, 43–44
    British relinquish, to
        United Nations, 58
    controlled entry to, 20
    kibbutzim in, 17–18
    partitioning of, 66–67
    prepares for German
        invasion, 56

rescued Jews sent to, 50, 51
Tamar prepares for, 26
Teddy on training farm in,
    18–19
Teddy receives permission
    to move to, 28
Teddy trains emigrants to,
    39–40
Zionist goals for, 12, 13, 16,
    47
Pomerantz, Venya, 53
Porush, Menahem, *89*

Rafi party, 78, 79, 80
Rothschild family, 7

Schallinger, Efra, 13, 29
Shemer, Naomi, 117
Six-Day War, 1–5, 90, 91, 97, 102
State of Israel. *See* Israel

Tel Aviv, 86
Tourism, in Israel, 70, 75–76

United Nations
    Britain relinquishes Palestine
        to, 58
    votes on division of Palestine,
        66–67

Vienna
    anti-Semitism in, 26
    after First World War, 10–11
    Jews in, 11

War of Independence, 70, 74, 84
Weizmann, Chaim, 43, *44*
Western Wall, 85

Zionism. *See also* Kollek, Teddy,
        in Zionist movement
    founding of, 12
    goals of, 12, 16–17
    pioneers of, 18